IF YOU'RE LUCKY,
YOUR HEART WILL BREAK

If You're Lucky, Your Heart Will Break

field notes from a Zen life

James Ishmael Ford

WISDOM PUBLICATIONS • BOSTON

Wisdom Publications
199 Elm Street
Somerville, MA 02144 USA
www.wisdompubs.org

"What to Look for When Looking for a Zen Teacher" originally appeared in *Zen Master WHO?* by James Ishmael Ford (Boston: Wisdom Publications, 2006) and is used by permission.

Library of Congress Cataloging-in-Publication Data

Ford, James Ishmael.
If you're lucky, your heart will break : field notes from a Zen life / James Ishmael Ford.
p. cm.
Includes index.
ISBN 1-61429-039-3 (pbk. : alk. paper)
1. Religious life—Zen Buddhism. I. Title.
BQ9286.2.F67 2012
294.3'927—dc23

2012006236

ISBN: 978-1-61429-039-1
eBook ISBN: 978-1-61429-043-8

16 15 14 13 12
5 4 3 2 1

Cover design by Phil Pascuzzo. The red seal on the cover appears courtesy of Boundless Way Zen. Author photo on page 185 is by Richard Boober. Interior design by Gopa&Ted2. Set in Sabon LT Std 10/14.2.

Wisdom Publications' books are printed on acid-free paper and meet the guidelines for permanence and durability of the Production Guidelines for Book Longevity of the Council on Library Resources.

Printed in the United States of America.

  This book was produced with environmental mindfulness. We have elected to print this title on 30% PCW recycled paper. As a result, we have saved the following resources: 12 trees, 5 million BTUs of energy, 1225 lbs. of greenhouse gases, 5526 gallons of water, and 350 lbs. of solid waste. For more information, please visit our website, www.wisdompubs.org. This paper is also FSC certified. For more information, please visit www.fscus.org.

For Jan Seymour-Ford

Let me respectfully remind you:
Life and death are of supreme importance.
Time swiftly passes by and opportunity is lost.
Each of us should strive to awaken... awaken!
Take heed!
Do not squander your life.

■ TRADITIONAL ZEN VERSE ■

Contents

Introduction

> I went to the woods because I wished to live deliber-
> ately, to front only the essential facts of life, and see if I
> could not learn what it had to teach, and not, when I
> came to die, discover that I had not lived.
>
> ■ HENRY DAVID THOREAU ■

AS BEST ANYONE KNOWS, the first Zen master to teach in the
West was the Japanese abbot Soyen Shaku. He was invited to
speak at the 1893 World Parliament of Religions in Chicago.
The roshi spoke little English, so his paper on causality, also
known as karma, was translated by his young student D.T.
Suzuki, and read by one of the parliament's organizers. The
paper received little attention from the press, but it did attract
the notice of the writer and publisher Paul Carus.

Carus and the roshi became friends, and through that
friendship some five years later the Zen master would return
to the United States and spend nine months based in California. While there, he taught the basic practices of Zen to
several people; among them was Ida Evelyn Russell, the first
Westerner of European descent I can ascertain to have taken
on koan introspection practice. In the little more than a hundred years that have passed since Soyen Shaku's visits laid
those first seeds into our rich Western loam, Zen has taken

root, perhaps tentatively and no doubt a little shallowly but also indisputably.

For me there is no tentativeness; the tendrils of this way have wound round and into my being and made me the person I am. What I write in the following pages represents the fruit of my Zen life. This is not an autobiography or memoir, but rather a deeply personal description of Zen teachings and central practices as best I understand them and as best I can present them. Most of all it is written for those who yearn for a way into genuine depth, for a map through the wastelands of the human heart and mind to our true home.

SADLY THE DHARMA IN THE WEST has divided along ethnic lines. Over the years communities of Asian immigrants have established themselves in the West, and while some of these Buddhist communities exist within an ethnic bubble, many do not. Among the most Western Buddhist communities primarily serving people of East Asian descent, I think immediately of the Buddhist Churches of America. The BCA has brought and adapted Pure Land Buddhism, creating a fascinating spiritual institution that can only be described as one of the predominant expressions of our emerging Western Dharma.

And this fact has frequently been missed. The majority of ethnic European descent converts have joined communities that are majority European descent, following trajectories ignorant of the evolution of Western Dharma within those communities established by Asian immigrants. I'm sure there are good reasons as well as bad for this, but I also believe this divide has been a wound in the Dharma come West.

And these divides continue.

Except for some intensely evangelical Lotus Sutra groups,

which have long had African-American membership, Americans of African descent are only now beginning to come to the Dharma in measurable numbers. The same has been true for people of Latino and Native American descent. We're just beginning to see a broadening of the attraction to the Dharma in the West.

My main point in raising all this, however, is that it would be a serious mistake to speak of these communities of European descent only as "Western Buddhism." I think the next generations coming along are more sensitive to these divides and, I think, more open to closing them. What I am seeing, is that whatever is coming as Western Buddhism is rich and getting richer.

As for me, I trained within the European descent bubble, although even there it is impossible to not be affected by, nor terribly grateful for, the influences of East Asian teachers and practitioners who brought the Dharma to us. My teacher's teachers were almost all immigrants from Japan or Japanese nationals who visited and were visited. How can I not have been touched? And as I eat with chopsticks several times a month, depending on what I'm eating, I see the cultural influences of the Buddha's many host cultures, meeting and challenging and melting and recreating, as well.

Today the great mix of American culture, particularly on the Western coast, is increasingly pan-Pacific. As I hope I've adequately said, I've been deeply touched by this. When I think of the African American, Native American and Latino cultural and spiritual perspective entering the conversation, I'm enormously excited, feeling I'm witnessing something very rich happening. Although the contours of what is forming are still unclear.

HERE IN THIS BOOK, I need to acknowledge what I bring to the table: I was raised a fundamentalist Christian of a Californian variety. I embraced a rational and humanist stance in my late adolescence and not much later I found Buddhism as it was presented among the first generation of European descent converts. Whatever its flaws, this presentation was authentic and rich. I was a Zen monk for several years in my young adulthood. For a variety of reasons, some of which I'll touch upon in this book, after that monastic experience I explored a variety of spiritual pathways, including visits with the Episcopal Church, the Gnostic traditions, and the Universalist Sufism taught by Hazrat Inayat Khan and Samuel Lewis and their heirs.

In my late thirties I settled down both physically and spiritually, finding the fullness of my life within Unitarian Universalism and Zen Buddhism. While this book is about Zen, my Zen is also informed by Unitarian Universalism and its institutions. I am a Zen priest, but I am also a UU minister and have spent twenty years serving in UU congregations. Accordingly, I think it important to offer a brief comment here on my perspective regarding Unitarian Universalism.

This emergent Western tradition is probably best called liberal religion. Western liberal religion has two hallmarks. One is a deep respect for reason and rationality. And the second is bringing a broadly humanist perspective to the matters of spirit, acknowledging that whatever else may be true of other worlds or realms, the work of religion is ultimately always here in this world. The great struggle for liberal religion is how best to manifest the broadest individual liberty while knowing that in the last analysis we exist only within relationships. This tradition and its struggles have proven a congenial home for many convert Western Buddhists—

particularly, through its comprehensive and open religious education programming, Western Buddhists with children. Though historically rooted in Christianity, Unitarian Universalism is not exactly a form of Christianity. I think that it has, through an independent evolution, come to stand in a place roughly between Taoism and Confucianism.

All this acknowledged I believe my stance can be summarized in calling myself a liberal Zen Buddhist. Today I am the heir to these two great traditions, and more as well. But essentially this means my Zen Buddhism is Western, mostly of the European-descent variety, flavored by my Christian upbringing, touched by the mystical traditions of the West and Near East, and very much informed by the great gift of the Western rational tradition. I've thrown myself into the way body, heart, and mind. I've found myself broken open and found in that opening my fundamental connection to the whole world, how we in our lives truly, truly are one.

As a Westerner of the rational inheritance, as I try to understand what I've experienced, I'm informed by a working assumption that if something is said to happen in the phenomenal world, I think it can be and should be subject to testing; and accordingly, I am eternally grateful for philosophical parsimony, the sharpness of Occam's Razor.

And at the same time I know a method is a method and not the goal of the questing heart. Not mixing these two things up has opened the way for me, and allowed me to reflect on this journey in ways that may be helpful to others who yearn for healing in this world of hurt.

The project of Zen and my engagement with it is about finding who I am, who we are as humans, and what is our true home. And that is what this book is about. Unitarian

Universalism and Zen Buddhism have brought me close to the great matter. At first I felt they complemented each other's weaknesses. Zen lacked institutions that made sense to me at the time, while Unitarian Universalism felt light on the spiritual side. Certainly, taken together I found a full life for myself. Today I cannot actually separate the two traditions; they have in a certain sense become one in my heart. There have been a number of consequences to this approach, of course, but on the whole still it has been a rich path to follow.

A great and useful gift I've found has been the ability we all share as human beings, to be able to step back a little, to place just enough distance between myself and my path, so that I am able to appreciate and sometimes appreciatively criticize this way that means so much to me, and which I think can mean so much for many people. Now, this is an important point. I did not find this gift by avoiding a full-hearted engagement with my path, but rather by using this very gift that we all have as human beings: that astonishing ability to watch ourselves. And, this is equally important; at the same time this way has invited me to let go of that distance at just the right moments.

I believe Zen is so important that it needs within it those who both love it passionately and also can see some of its flaws and shadows. As a human institution presenting a cluster of insights discovered by human beings, and offering a small package of disciplines also cultivated by human beings, of course it is flawed. The only questions are how flawed—and how helpful?

I threw myself into the Zen way to find out the most important things about who I am and what I might be, always looking at the path itself as well as my own heart and mind. What follows is what I have to offer: the results of that life and a description of the way for those who are similarly drawn to a rigorous investigation of the spiritual life, who are seeking nothing watered down, or attenuated. Just honesty. Only the real deal, only the truth—as best I have found it.

PART I

What Is Awakening?

Then the Divine answered Job out of the whirlwind,
and said: "Who is this who despairs without knowledge? Pull yourself together. I have questions for
you, and you must answer. Where were you when I
laid the foundations of the earth? Tell me, if you
understand. Who measured out the universe?—do
you understand? Who gave it shape?—do you
understand? Who set the foundation, who set down
the cornerstone? When the morning stars sang
together, and all the children of God shouted for joy,
where were you?"

■ JOB 38:1–7 ■

The Answer, Sort of

I'VE BEEN WALKING THE ZEN WAY for the larger part of a lifetime. And along this way of terrible broken hearts and unspeakable joys, of learning what a fool I usually am, and of a wondrous beauty that pervades the entire world and invades the hearts of people—even people as difficult as me—I've learned a few things about this Zen way that may be worth sharing.

The first is that it is all oversold a bit. There is indeed such a thing as enlightenment, as awakening, absolutely; I've tasted awakening in small and large ways. But what enlightenment actually is isn't quite as grand as the literature sometimes suggests. Or, rather, it is considerably subtler and more dynamic than we ever think. Actually, as one Zen teacher said, "Awakening isn't what you think." Quite simply, awakening (a term I generally prefer to *enlightenment*) is part and parcel of our human condition. It doesn't take us outside of the natural realm to any other place—awakening is found within our lives, just as they are.

THERE IS A KOAN, a traditional Zen teaching story, that addresses this. This koan appears in the twelfth-century

Chinese anthology the *Wumenguan*, the *Gateless Gate*, case 2:

THE MASTER BAIZHANG HUAIHAI gave a series of talks on the Dharma. Among those who attended was an old man who sat near the back of the hall. One day the old man lingered after the talk and the master approached him, asking, "Who are you?"

The old man replied, "Many eons ago I was the master of a Zen temple on this spot. One day a sincere student of the way asked me whether someone who had awakened was bound by the laws of cause and effect, or not. I replied 'No, such a person is not tangled in the strands of causality.' Ever since that time I've been reborn as a fox. Perhaps five hundred times now. I'm desperately hoping you can say that turning word and free me from this horrible fate."

He then made formal bows before the master and asked the question. "Is someone who has experienced awakening bound by the laws of cause and effect, or not?"

The master replied, "Such a person is one with the laws of cause and effect."

Hearing this, the old man responded, "Thank you, those words have liberated me. I am released from this fox body. I have just one more request. My body is around the other side of the mountain. Can you retrieve it and give it a monk's burial?"

Baizhang agreed and when the spirit vanished he called the head monk and announced that after the noon meal there would be a funeral. This information passed like wildfire through the assembly. Everyone knew there was no one in the infirmary, so they were very curious. After the meal the monks made their way around the mountain, retrieved the fox's body, returned to the monastery, and gave it a priest's interment.

Later that evening the master told the assembly what had happened.

His student Huangbo stepped forward and asked, "Master, what if when asked about awakening and causality he had given the right answer? What then?"

Baizhang smiled and said, "Come here and I'll tell you."

Baizhang was a very small man, but his teacher's stick was sitting in his lap, and the wise avoided his reach. Huangbo was said to be seven feet tall so as he walked up to his teacher he came within his very long arm's reach while still well short of his teacher's; Huangbo reached out and slapped the master.

Baizhang laughed and laughed, and said to the assembly, "I thought the founder of our way, Bodhidharma, the barbarian from the West, had a red beard. But right here with us is a red-bearded barbarian!"

FOR THOSE ENGAGED in the discipline of Zen koan introspection, this is a complicated case with several important points to investigate. For our purposes here, I want simply to draw your attention to how, in the story, the old master of that mountain had been tangled in the all-too-common idea that awakening/enlightenment somehow excuses us from life. It doesn't.

The awakened person is one with the flow of cause and effect, is one with the play of life and death, is the same person who has longings and desires, who is hurt and who needs. With awakening we are in all respects the same people we've always been, woven out of the mess of genes and history, our stuff the stuff of the world. But with this truth we are awakened to the reality of our intimate connections.

As we proceed here, what this actually means will be explored from a number of angles.

The grand language that one runs across within our Zen literature is appropriate because it points to a fundamental shift in human consciousness that does indeed liberate us from fear and shows us just how intimately connected we are with this whole great, lovely, and terrible matter that is life—and death.

It is about being real; not more real, not less.

Awake or not, or (as we actually usually live) now awake, now not; each step we take, each action we engage, each word that tumbles from our lips, and actually each thought that forms in our heads creates conditions that will engage with other conditions, and will have consequences. Everything is connected and everything has consequences.

As a practical matter this spiritual project is an invitation to discover who we really are. As such it is encountered, engaged and manifested entirely within our lives. As we open to this larger perspective we find a certain grace, and a whole new world of possibility.

Awakening does not particularly address the hurt of our childhoods nor does it fix our relationships with each other or the world. In fact I suggest that most of us who wish to embark on the spiritual quest would wisely also find competent psychological counseling. They can go together quite nicely.

Similarly, following the spiritual path doesn't require going into a monastery—not that that is a bad thing for those so inclined. In fact for the right person it can be the wisest thing in the world. But the monastic way isn't how most of us are going to live, and to think it necessary can be a bad mistake. Rather, I encourage everyone who walks the spiritual way to find a kind of work that is fulfilling and to pursue the proper preparation for being employed at doing it, whether that is going to welding school or getting a teacher's certificate or, God help you, going to seminary as I did. Don't put off your life. The spiritual, the worldly—it is all one thing.

Informed by our experience of awakening, we can more healthily engage those things. We can use the light that shines when we open our hearts and minds to discover our larger identity, to walk more carefully, more wisely on this sweet and suffering planet.

Earthquakes

THE FIRST HALF OF 2010 felt like the year of the earthquake. In January Haiti was absolutely devastated; in February there was another, even stronger quake in Chile, although fortunately less damaging; in March another tumbler in Taiwan; quickly followed by one more in Mexico; then in April, a pretty bad one on the Tibetan plateau. No doubt, such things can give one pause.

Among the responses to the devastation of these events was New Age guru Dr. Deepak Chopra sending a tweet to his followers, apologizing for starting the quake in Mexico through the force of his meditations. I assumed it was a joke—if one in pretty bad taste. But when asked for clarification, the good doctor didn't plead an unfortunate sense of humor; instead he explained that he'd indeed been doing a powerful meditation at the time of the quake, though he did acknowledge that correlation isn't necessarily causation.

As creepy as that might be, however, it pales when compared to fundamentalist Christian preacher Pat Robertson's astonishing assertion that the horrendous Haitian earthquake was the result of Haiti's founders having made a pact with the devil. "Blame the victim" is a venerable if reprehensible tradition explaining horrors, natural and otherwise.

Of course both these characters stand in a long line of people getting out in front of disasters and suggesting they know why they happened. The ones above are classic examples: one to claim unseen powers, another to blame the victim—though blaming victims is a way to claim power, as well. And these sorts of responses are about power—who has it, and who doesn't.

And these are among the reasons I'm not overly enamored with religions.

Too often it's just about power. No doubt natural disasters are very powerful things—and few are as mysterious and confusing and frightening as earthquakes. As a native Californian, I know—I've experienced many quakes. By and large, for most of my life, I didn't really give them a lot of thought—until, that is, October 1989.

My wife Jan and I were living in Berkeley, California. On October 17, at 5:04 PM, I was at my internship site at the First Unitarian Church in San Jose, at the bottom of the Bay some forty-five miles from Berkeley. The whole thing remains vivid in my mind. I was standing in the front office, as was Lindi, our senior minister. Margie, our church's administrator, was sitting at her desk. That's when the earthquake struck. We were all native Californians so we ignored the first pitch. But with the second roll, as products of California's public education system, Lindi and I each stepped into doorways while Margie went under her desk.

And that's when I realized there was something they didn't mention in those instructions at school. It was true I was in a relatively secure place should the building collapse—but I was also sharing that space with a door that wanted to fly back and forth. At 6.9 on the Richter scale and known later as the "pretty big one," the Loma Prieta remains one of the largest recorded earthquakes in the lower forty-eight, and the most severe quake either Jan or I have ever experienced.

While I was in San Jose sharing space with that door, Jan was up in Berkeley in our apartment, ironing and listening to records. The room she was in, as were all our rooms in that small apartment, was filled with jerry-rigged bookshelves reaching from floor nearly to the ceiling on every wall. She felt one sharp jolt. A book fell off one shelf. As we were the building managers, Jan went outside to see if the earthquake valve—a mechanical device that turns the gas flowing into a building off at any severe jolt—had been thrown. It hadn't, so she returned to her ironing. It would be an hour or so later when she turned on the radio before she learned why I wasn't about to walk through the door.

Turns out that our neighborhood sat on a solid hunk of granite, and a big one at that. However, this wasn't true for most of the rest of the Bay Area, which had experienced a hellish fifteen seconds. There were sixty-two deaths; nearly four thousand people were hurt; parts of several freeways—including one that I drove along pretty nearly every day—and a section of the Bay Bridge collapsed; eighteen thousand homes were damaged; and a total estimated six billion dollars were lost in those fifteen seconds. That's power.

And Jan and I, like so many others, were left shaken to the core. I can't quite describe the feeling after such an experience. The fragility of it all, and the tentativeness of life itself, seemed to seep into our pores, and grew slowly from the first exhilaration of having made it, to a bone-and-marrow knowing that the earth could move from under us at any time, and no place really was safe, no place. The next year when I was offered a call to serve a church in Wisconsin, despite being Californians who had never lived outside the boundaries of our native state, Jan and I were pretty happy to leave earthquake country.

And I've found I have a take-away from that experience: I find myself thinking a lot about how the lessons that stick tend to be the ones that catch me off guard, that knock me out of my safety zones. They can be big, and they can be small. These experiences, big and small, are all intimations of what we really are.

Paul Evans, who blogs as "Melville at the Custom-House" provides a nice example of what that small intimation might look like:

> Panhandlers frequented most of the main streets in Clifton, the neighborhood in Cincinnati where I lived from 1990 until 1995. They were quite a nuisance, especially when they set up shop by ATMs and pay phones. I made it a point to never make eye contact or acknowledge them.
>
> One night, a bearded street person in his mid-60s came up to me and actually clutched my sleeve. "Young man, do you have money for dinner?" They always needed it for a cup of coffee, or bus fare, or for a meal—never to buy booze. That was how cynical I was.
>
> "No, I don't," I said, using a tone that telegraphed to him the matter was not open for discussion.
>
> "Well, for God's sake, get yourself something!" he said, stuffing a five-dollar bill in the breast pocket of my shirt. Before I could fully comprehend what had just happened, he disappeared in the other direction.

I queried Paul and he assured me the person was almost certainly indigent: his clothes needed cleaning, and so did he. I've been thinking about that, and the small earthquake for my new friend. And what it has meant for him in the days and weeks and years since.

I found myself thinking of that old Yiddish saying: "God is not nice. God is not your uncle. God is an earthquake."

WE ALL CAN MAKE OURSELVES the center of the universe a bit too easily, and start seeing everything that is going on as being about us, about *me*. Like Dr. Chopra "causing" the earthquake. There is danger in this way of thinking. The truth is that in most of life, most of our lives, most of us are walk-ons, minor characters at best, with a single line to say.

But we can also, like my friend and that poor man who gave him five dollars, let the encounter open us up like a flower in bloom. It is at such moments—when I just open up, when my heart is thrown open in spite of myself—in which I discover the beginnings of meaning. Not *meaning* in the sense of an Aristotelian thread of argument, but *meaning* as something powerful and compelling, and for our human hearts maybe more important than the solution to a problem.

This sense of deep meaning is the sense that informs the Yiddish saying above: the earthquake upsets what we expect and gives us something else, something quite possibly devastating. I suggest this isn't so much even about letting go, but about discovering there is nothing to hold on to, and nor has there ever been.

This is about being thrown into the chaos of it all, of being swept away.

IN THIS CONTEXT I'd like to hold up the *Book of Job* for your consideration. I've wrestled with that book for ages and have come back to its points on any number of occasions. I've found in that ancient book how, in the midst of suffering and longing and frustrated desire, in the midst of that deafening silence to our pleas and calls, we are in fact given a gift. It is a terrible gift, no doubt. The wounds we receive in our lives, the death of children, the ravages of disease, the hunger and want that haunt this world—in addition to the horror of their reality—that moment of confusion and uncertainty can also open our hearts to some fearful reality, some astonishing reality.

I'm not calling for a joyful embrace here; at least not exactly. One would be right in raging against the horror of such things as follow in the wake of these earthquakes. Indeed there is an almost endless litany of things in life that should offend us. But, in addition to weeping for the children, and doing our best to work to help the survivors— we can also look full on, and not turn away. And if we do, if we really do not turn away from those hurts, we find something.

We discover that who we are counts, however important or not we might be in the ordering of things. We discover that what we are as individuals is in fact holy. But, it is a terrible holiness. After all that happens to Job, after his great demand for justice, then, there, from out of the whirlwind— or, you can just as easily say from within the earthquake— he and we get the gift of a terrible presence and a roaring confrontation with all that is.

It is that which pulls out of Job his hymn, "I have spoken of the unspeakable and tried to grasp the infinite... I had heard of you with my ears; but now my eyes have seen you. Therefore I will be quiet, comforted that I am dust."

Comforted that I am dust. This passage has long haunted people. Some rage against it, saying all that Job is doing is wallowing in that dust, squeaking his submission to the great cosmic bully. But I suggest there is more here. That wise commentator on this whole great mess, Stephen Mitchell, in his modern spiritual classic, *The Book of Job*, tells us, "Job's comfort at the end is in his mortality."

So we need to be appalled at what has happened. We need to reach out a hand to those in need. We need to stop, to notice, and to discover in this terrible moment something about ourselves. It is, I suggest, the gateway to wisdom. And that is where we find meaning, purpose, and direction, which is also our work, perhaps the great work itself.

Out of the earthquakes of our lives, small and great—in the awe, in the silence that follows—notice.

Everything follows this noticing.

Every Day Is a Good Day

> Yunmen taught, "I do not ask you about before the fif-
> teenth of the month. Come, say something about after
> the fifteenth." And then he responded for himself,
> "Every day is a good day."
>
> ■ BLUE CLIFF RECORD, CASE 6 ■

ON AUGUST 6, 2005—among other things the sixtieth
anniversary of the bombing of Hiroshima—I was given *inka
shomei* by my principal Zen teacher, John Tarrant. This the
final formal authorization a teacher of Zen receives. *Inka
shomei* is a Japanese phrase that roughly translates as "the
legitimate seal of clearly furnished proof"—or, according
to another teacher whom I greatly respect, "Show me the
ink!" It is a public acknowledgment—to my mind less of
accomplishment, and more of possibility—that I might actually be able to help people on the Zen way.

It is also conventional for someone who has been given
inka to give a talk on a particular koan. *Koan* means, per
Robert Aitken's definition, "a presentation of the universal
and the particular; a theme of Zen to be made clear." And
the particular koan that is traditionally addressed at this special time comes from a twelfth-century Chinese anthology
called the *Biyan Lu*, in Japanese the *Hekiganroku*, and in

English, the Blue Cliff Record: case 6, usually called "Every Day Is a Good Day."

In a tradition not known for indulging in positive thinking—a tradition in fact known for rubbing our noses in what life actually presents, however difficult or unpleasant it might be—this can prove to be something of a difficult text. I didn't give that talk at my inka ceremony, but rather gave it the next day at the First Unitarian Society of Newton, which I served at that time as Senior Minister; I chose to preach using Yunmen's words as my text. Considering my life, it felt right that my first formal talk after receiving inka would be from the pulpit of the Unitarian Universalist congregation I was serving.

The text of the case appears in full as an epigraph to this chapter, and it is pretty simple. Here it is again:

Yunmen taught, "I do not ask you about before the fifteenth of the month. Come, say something about after the fifteenth." And then he responded for himself, "Every day is a good day."

This isn't quite as esoteric as it might at first sound. In the ancient Chinese calendar the fifteenth of the month is the time of the full moon. And the full moon is one of the ancient symbols for awakening. So, the question Yunmen is asking may also be phrased, "I don't ask about before your awakening, but rather I want you to speak out of your awakening." Obviously there's still some unpacking to do. Let's start with context.

Yunmen Wenyan was one of the greatest of China's Zen masters, living from the middle of the ninth century into the middle of the tenth. This was the time when the Tang dynasty collapsed into what is called the period of the Five Dynasties and the Ten States—a period of nearly continuous warfare and horrific social upheaval. Yunmen towered above this terrible time, a beacon of light within the darkness. An amazing figure, he occurs throughout the literature of Zen, appearing dozens of times in the great classic collections of anecdotes and sayings of the masters.

In our time Andy Ferguson has compiled his own magnificent collection of the sayings and doings of the first generations of Zen masters in his book *Zen's Chinese Heritage*. There he records the story of Yunmen's awakening, which I find directly relevant to any investigation of the assertion "Every day is a good day." After years of diligent study under a variety of teachers, Yunmen went to see the master Muzhou Daoming. Muzhou was famously cranky, and would often shut the door of his hut as soon as he heard someone approach down the path. And, indeed, as Yunmen came to his hut, Muzhou closed his door.

> Yunmen knocked on the door.
> Muzhou said, "Who is it?"
> Yunmen said, "It's me."
> Muzhou said, "What do you want?"
> Yunmen said, "I'm not clear about my life. I'd like the master to give me some instruction."
> Muzhou then opened the door and, taking a look at Yunmen, closed it again. Yunmen knocked on the door in this manner three days in a row. On the third day when Muzhou opened the door, Yunmen stuck his foot in the doorway.
> Muzhou grabbed Yunmen and yelled, "Speak! Speak!" When Yunmen began to speak, Muzhou gave him a shove and said, "Too late!"
> Muzhou then slammed the door, catching and

breaking Yunmen's foot. At that moment, Yunmen experienced enlightenment.

He carried the mark of his enlightenment, his awakening, for the rest of his life—along with a foot that never quite
healed. Frankly, I myself much prefer a certificate, and I
thank my teacher that it is so nice. The question really, however, is was what Yunmen experienced worth the years of
struggle, the burning pain of that encounter, and the lifetime limp that followed? What was it that led him to assert
out of his awakening that every day is a good day?

I suggest his point isn't prosaic; it's more complicated than
just saying yes to what is. In fact he's taking us to a place we
cannot go while clinging to ideas of high or low, good or ill.
What is being pointed to all turns on the Zen teaching of
awakening. So let's hold that up for a moment. One Japanese word for the instant of awakening is *kensho*, which literally means "seeing into one's nature." Another word for this
is *satori*, which derives from a verb meaning "to know." Here
we're addressing a particular kind of religious or spiritual
experience—not a philosophical assertion, as I need to underscore and underscore again. Yunmen points to an accessible
insight into what it is we can know and how we can know it.

Everything here is about living, about breathing, about
being. Zen asserts how reality as we can perceive it is two
things simultaneously. On the one side is what I'd call the
world of history, the world of things emergent. This is what
we commonly sense and understand: I am here, you are
there. Each and every thing exists in its own trajectory and
you and I are definitely not the same. However, at the same
time, simultaneously, in an offense to Aristotle and, perhaps,
to common sense, Zen asserts how you and I and all the

cosmos, every precious bit within that realm of history, of things emergent, share something in common.

From this angle on reality, you might say we all, you and I, have no top, no bottom. We appear in the world, quite real, but without finite edges. Turns out we are not complete and autonomous; rather we bleed out into the universe, into openness. Or perhaps it's better to say we arise out of, are sustained by, and return to that openness, that boundlessness. A traditional Zen word for this aspect of what we are is "empty." You might think of this *empty* as our family name. You and I, and flies and lice, and stars and planets, and heat and cold—those are our personal names. But we also all belong to the great Empty family.

In one Zen text, Hakuin's *Song of Zazen*, we are told that our condition of drifting along cut off from our birthright, from our Empty family, is like "a child of a wealthy home wandering among the poor." This is important. What we're addressing isn't a philosophical assertion. It is a spiritual assertion. It's about, when all is said and done, who and what we are. It's about our true heritage. And, happily, within the Zen way, this assertion comes with an invitation.

You and I can know this truth for ourselves as our own personal truth. Just like when we take a drink of water we know intimately and immediately whether it is cool or warm. So we can know the assertion that we are one even as we are many in some way that helps, genuinely helps. And, Yunmen asserts, there is something of joy and peace and possibility in this knowing. Although, I have to admit, it isn't exactly a knowing; knowing, after all, belongs to the dualism of knowing and not knowing. And we're going somewhere else.

I believe we can get a hint about that somewhere else

through a look at Yunmen's "good day." This is not an assertion that denies the mess of life, that says that the nearly
two hundred thousand lives lost directly and indirectly in
the bombing of Hiroshima, for instance, didn't happen, and
wasn't horrible. Nor is it an assertion about the awfulness,
wars and terrors that are going on today.

Well, not exactly.

Yunmen, lame and living in the midst of war and famine,
asks his community to address that time after awakening.
And from that place he answers on our behalf that "every
day is a good day." Two points flow at this moment. One is
practical if, for our purposes here, secondary: If we discover
our true family name as the deepest truth about ourselves,
then our actions in the world of personal names will become
a little more skillful. But primarily, there is the first point:
Why think you're separate, alone, isolated if it isn't true?
How can you find out—for yourself, like taking that drink
of water—that you are vastly greater than your imagining?
How do you get there?

Well, *there* is actually right here. We find it, you and I, as
we learn to open our hands rather than to hold too tightly,
crushing the life out of things. We learn as we sit down, shut
up, and pay attention. Or, in the gentler words of my friend,
the Zen teacher Diane Rizzetto: stop, attend, listen. It's that
easy. No more difficult than falling off a log. Just for a
moment, let go of your ideas about *what is* and let *what is*
be. Forget Zen Buddhist. Forget Christian, or Jew or Mus-
lim or Hindu. Forget *like*. Forget *dislike*.

Forget, just for a second, just for a single beat of the heart.

My goodness, at that moment, if you're just a little lucky,
your heart will break, the parties of your inner war will
declare an armistice, and with Yunmen and all the ances-

tors of the Great Way your mouth will open and you will sing the truth of the heavens and the earth. It is the amazing grace that fills the world, and births hope in every moment.

That's when we can stand with Job, covered in dust, take it all in, and declare with the fullness of our hearts the great truth.

Every day is a good day.

After which we can get up, dust ourselves off, and get on with the work that is calling—the many tasks, small and large, to which our hearts call us.

PART II

Sit Down, Shut Up, and Pay Attention

The way is originally perfect and all-pervading; how could it be contingent on practice and realization? The true vehicle is self-sufficient; what need is there for special effort? Indeed, the whole body is free from dust; who could believe in a means to brush it clean?

■ EIHEI DOGEN ■

On Having a Spiritual Practice

MANY YEARS AGO I was living in a Zen Buddhist monastery in Oakland, California. We sat in formal Zen meditation for several hours every day, except during the monthly retreats when we sat for ten or eleven hours each day—and if you've never tried it, I should say that is physically challenging. In fact it involves a certain consistent level of pain. However, I don't recall much of the sitting, nor of the pain. Nor do I recall the liturgical life in any detail, nor the formal study, nor even the regular round of work. What I do recall, vividly, is how I was always hungry.

One evening I was eating a thin vegetable soup, feeling seriously sorry for myself. How in the world had I gotten myself into such a mess? Perhaps late that night I would simply pack my belongings, didn't have too many of those to worry about, and slip away. Or, at least I could go to the nearest taqueria. And I knew of one just a few blocks away. A nice big beef burrito would certainly hit the spot.

Of course the practice was paying attention. Attending while sitting in meditation, yes, but also attending while working, while reading, while doing everything, including, of course, and very much so, eating. So reluctantly I drew myself back from that little reverie involving refried beans, sautéed vegetables, pulled spiced beef, pico de gallo, and maybe just a hint of guacamole, and returned to my thin, thin soup.

I'd quickly eaten all the vegetables and all that was left was—have I mentioned?—a very thin broth, but with a miso base, so cloudy I couldn't see to the bottom of the bowl. I stirred absently, watching small whirls of clouds appear and disappear in the soup. Another wave of regret and sorrow washed over me. But again I returned to the moment, to attending to the meal, such as it was, in front of me. As I just looked, a cabbage leaf floated up to the surface. I was ecstatic, absolutely ecstatic.

Then something magical happened. As I just watched, I had this amazing sense of gratitude for that cabbage leaf. And I felt gratitude for my companions in this strange project to which I'd committed myself. Then I was aware of our neighbors in the city and of the city itself. I felt gratitude for them and the people of the state and the country and the globe.

I felt a sense of joy wash through the cosmos itself. And then there I was, just me looking at that cabbage leaf. There was only that cabbage leaf floating there in front of me. No stories about it, no stories about me. Just this. Nothing more. I slipped the cabbage leaf onto my spoon, raised it to my mouth and ate it.

The gratitude was a set up. The payoff was just slipping the cabbage leaf onto the spoon, just that motion, then raising it to my mouth, just that raising, just that moment. And just eating. Just this. Just this. The words, oh God, the words fail. But the consequences have played out for a lifetime.

It was just a taste. But it was, for me, the taste of awakening.

Awakening happens.

You don't earn it. You don't have to be good. You don't have to be smart. Awakening just happens.

And it comes to us in surprising places and times, sometimes while meditating or on retreat, or slurping down a cabbage leaf, but actually a bit more likely while washing dishes, or chasing an errant three-year-old, or sitting on the toilet.

Awakening comes to us in the most unexpected ways, in the most unexpected times. It is a gift. It is always a gift. And it comes to us like being hit by a bus.

There are many, many practices out there that claim to help. And here's a little secret: too many of them do nothing. The Unitarian Universalist theologian James Luther Adams once wryly noted how "Nothing sells like egoism wrapped in idealism." Much of what passes for spiritual practice is just puffing up the ego, reinforcing and guarding it against any and all assault. And—have no doubt in this matter—a real spiritual practice plays rough with the ego.

And the Zen path is, in this regard and others, a real spiritual practice. And it is worth pursuing, wholeheartedly. But keep your wits about you, be reasonable. Don't exaggerate any one experience. And, equally important, don't diminish it, either. Engage it all with a spirit of invitation, and maybe you'll begin to notice gratitude welling up from somewhere deep within. Whatever, somehow, your insight will appear, your awakening, your gate into the wide world and your initiation into knowing you truly are part of the great Empty family.

Have a little courage and maintain some diligence. Diligence is important.

Once I was in a meeting of Zen teachers and we were discussing what defines a real practice. One of the teachers wanted to express the finest and the highest, to outline a way that encompassed the whole of a life. It was rather beautiful. And I was more than passingly annoyed. I'm more petty, small minded. I want to know what the minimums are. Sadly, what I've come to see is that there is no one who can tell a person what exactly must be done in order to harvest the possibilities of Zen practice. There are just too many variables to make any one-size-fits-all assertion.

Here's a hard fact. Just sitting once a week is not a Zen practice. It's true that you might wake up with that one sit. But I wouldn't put a lot of money on that likelihood. I think for most of us sitting a minimum of about a half an hour a day, most days of the week, is the baseline. And if you can also throw in some retreats—half-day, full-day, multi-day— once in a while, that's generally even better. The majority of serious Zen practitioners do more than this. But I also need to hold this up: some who have truly found the Zen way in their own hearts do less.

But be careful. Doing less than this, particularly at the beginning, when trying to find your way into Zen, sets up the distinct possibility of a dilettante practice, growing something with no roots and little chance of fruition. And, again, no one knows precisely what makes a real Zen practice, at least in terms of how much is enough. So, bottom line: just do your best. And when you find you're not, which is what most of us have experienced, often over and over, just pick yourself up, dust yourself off, and start again.

The way is vast and endlessly forgiving.

It is also harsh, demanding everything from us. But this "everything" is not about how much time you choose to put on the pillow.

Now, the truth is that even getting to that half-hour a day can be difficult. While this is changing, there are still relatively few places in the country where one can find a center that offers a place to sit on a daily basis. I have little doubt that would be the best way to do it. I was blessed with living in an area with multiple centers where I could sit on just about any day of the week. And there's an amazing power in sitting with others. But looking around North America there aren't that many such centers. Most likely if one finds a center it is going to offer a sitting opportunity once a week. So use it. And cultivate your own practice.

At the beginning, I recommend that regularity is vastly more important than duration. So, if you determine to sit three days a week for ten minutes a shot, and you do it, you're on your way. I've met too many people who, caught in the passion of the moment, declare they will sit two hours a day for the rest of their lives. They don't. And often, embarrassed, they disappear.

Stretch a little beyond what seems comfortable.

Sit at least a little most every day.

And plod on.

Forgive yourself your failures, but resume. Fall down, pick yourself up, dust yourself off, and start over again. One teacher liked to say "Fall down nine times, get up ten." Start over.

That's the practice.

Beginning

A MILLION YEARS AGO, or so, I decided to try Zen meditation. I'd been shopping for a spiritual practice for a while. And in the San Francisco Bay Area of the 1960s that meant I had lots of options. I tried a number of them. But nothing really caught me. But all the time people kept saying, "You should check out the Zen Center." They meant the San Francisco Zen Center.

I'd heard all sorts of things about the master over there, Shunryu Suzuki. Many of the things I'd heard were unlikely, some ridiculous. But people also talked about his gentleness and quiet wisdom; these were rare among the spiritual teacher types I had been encountering. I was told he only taught one practice, something called "zazen." Which I was told meant "seated Zen." As my understanding was that *Zen* simply meant meditation, it appeared that zazen was some kind of meditation one did sitting down. I figured I could do that.

The center was actually a temple housed in a former synagogue in Japantown. First, while wandering around the outside of the building, I accidentally wandered through a door into a lower room where some elderly Japanese men were playing a game of *go*. They didn't seem all that happy a young hippy interrupted them, but they told me how to find my way to the front entrance where the Zen happened.

Later I would come to learn that there was some tension between the Japanese congregation that had brought the roshi over from Japan to serve as their pastor and paid his salary, and the increasing numbers of young people who came to practice Zen. At the time all I thought was, "Hmm, *go*. Perhaps I should learn that, too. If this Zen thing works out." I began to fantasize about what a Japanese-inspired life might look like. I figured it had to be better than what I had; the psychedelic dream of the '60s was beginning to fall apart for me. I knew there had to be a better way. I hoped this would be it.

A priest named Claude Dahlenberg gave the small group collected there that morning the basics. We were taught how to sit on the traditional pillow, the zafu, which was small and round and, in those days, always stuffed with kapok, a fibrous material that looked a bit like raw cotton. We were shown how to place our bottoms on the front half of the pillow, which caused our legs to naturally fall forward, inclining our knees toward the ground. For those of us able to get our knees all the way to the floor, maybe three of the seven there for the class, this created a triangular base that supported the torso, which we were told should be held upright. As we sat, our knees and ankles were supported by a second pillow, a larger square of batted cotton called a zabuton upon which both the zafu and meditator rested. In the Japanese style both pillows were black.

We were told the ideal way to sit would be in the full lotus—with each leg folded so the foot rested atop the opposite thigh. None of us could do this. So we were shown how to do various modifications: the half lotus with only one foot resting on a thigh and the other placed on the ground slightly forward; the quarter lotus (which, Claude sniffed, was some-

times called the "half-assed lotus") where the single foot
rested on the calf rather than the thigh; or finally, the way I
more or less could sit, where the ankles simply were set one
in front of the other in what is called the Burmese style.

At the time we weren't told that sometimes people kneel,
using that pillow set sideways, or with a special bench. Nor
were we told many people also simply sit in chairs. So long
as one's bottom is higher than one's knees, by placing the
feet flat on the ground one can get that same triangular support for the torso.

Since then, I've learned that the most important thing is
to try and sit upright, with the back "straight"—that is, with
that gentle s-curve that the spine naturally takes. If one does
this properly with adequate support, usually in one of those
variations on the lotus posture, the back can sit like that for
quite long periods of time.

Some people have real problems with the aches and pains
involved, particularly the pain that can occur in the knees.
There is a balance here. On the one hand we shouldn't be
afraid of a little pain. It comes naturally enough in life. And
a spiritual practice that doesn't ask you to push a bit through
pain isn't a real spiritual practice. But there is also romanc-
ing the pain, a sort of spiritual masochism, which needs to
be guarded against. In all things seek the middle way. Push,
but not too hard. This is also one of those areas where it is
important to have a community of practice and a competent guide, people who are familiar with what is going on,
and can help.

There are those who claim one can only practice Zen while
sitting in some prescribed manner, sitting upright in one of
those variations on the lotus. This simply is not true. Early
on in my practice I met a woman who was a quadriplegic.

At that time she was a very senior student and had passed most of the koans in the Harada-Yasutani koan system—which meant by Zen standards she'd had that awakening experience and probably refined it substantially. And, of course, she never ever sat upright in the conventional sense. Never had, never would.

After the other novice students and I had struggled into whatever posture we could, we were shown how to hold our hands in our laps in a posture called the "cosmic mudra." We were instructed on how to place our tongue in our mouths, with it resting easily against the upper palate and with our upper and lower teeth touching lightly, but not clenching. And we were told to sit with our eyes partially open, and with our gaze falling to the ground a couple of feet in front of us. Years later I would hear a teacher, when asked whether one should meditate with their eyes open or closed, reply, "Personally, I like to see where I'm going." This eyes-open style is rare among meditators in other traditions, but the normative practice among Zen sitters, as Zen meditators are often called.

Then we were told to count our breaths. In the time since then, I've learned there are many ways to count one's breath.

OFTEN THE PRACTICE involves manipulation of the breath. And sometimes a mantra is introduced. For instance in the Kwan Um School, a Korean style of Zen, most beginners are instructed to breathe in on a count of three while also attaching the phrase "clear mind." Then exhale for a count of seven, attaching the phrase "don't know." In both the inhalation and the exhalation the phrases "clear mind" and "don't know" should occupy the full of the count.

The neuroscientist and Zen practitioner James Austin suggests a somewhat simpler adaptation of the use of a mantra for counting the breath in his study *Selfless Insight*. He recommends the phrase "just this." It has two parts and requires some attention. For the first ten breath cycles, as you inhale say "just" and as you exhale count one. Repeat ten times, changing the number to two, three, and so on. Then, for the next ten breath cycles, as you inhale say "this" and exhale with the counts, repeating ten times. During all this he suggests an awareness of the abdomen's motions with the in and out breaths. As one sinks into the depths of the meditation, let the practice shift, simply allowing "just" to occupy the inhalation and "this" the exhalation.

Professor Austin points out this is an expedient. "Later, it, too, dissolves into the breathing movements of the lower abdomen and vanishes like any other concept." Not long ago I was visiting a member of the congregation I was serving, someone I am quite fond of, who was facing a pretty hard diagnosis. She was not a meditator, but now under these circumstances asked if I had a mantra that might be useful. I recalled Professor Austin's meditative schema and suggested she say "just" as she inhaled and "this" as she exhaled. We did it together for a while, and it had a powerful effect for her, and for me.

That long ago Saturday morning in the old synagogue, we were instructed to take five breath cycles and number each inhalation and each exhalation. So, inhale: one. Exhale: two. Inhale: three. And so on to ten, and then to start over again. I recommend this as the simplest of the breath counting systems.

At the time, we weren't given a lot of additional instruction. It turns out counting to ten over and over can be pretty hard. The mind just wanders. And don't let anyone tell you that you can actually "stop" the mind. There is only one way to stop it, and that one way isn't generally a happy option for people. You can slow it down. There are moments of crystal clarity and profound silence. But always somewhere, deep down, the mind moves. And it really moves at the beginning of the discipline, when we first try to stop and notice. So, over the years I learned that some people find it easier to take up the whole breath with the number. Mentally count *ooooooone* for however long it takes to inhale. Then *twoooooo* for however long it takes to exhale. And so on.

As I said, attending to one's breath and counting inhalations and exhalations can be quite a project. One loses count. One counts robotically; I once got up to thirty-six before noticing. The deal is to notice the distraction and to return to one.

The heart of the discipline: notice and start over.

Turns out there are three principal variations on distraction. The first is to notice one has been distracted and then to blame the environment. "It is too noisy outside." "The kids are too loud." "My neighbor's belly is making horrible noises." Of course to get into ascribing responsibility for the distraction is simply a meta-distraction. The deal is to notice the distraction and to return to one. Just start over.

Another variation in that meta-distraction is to rebuke oneself. "I'm not smart enough." "I don't have enough discipline." Of course this is simply a variation on blame, turning the blame inside rather than outside. Notice. Start over.

And then there's the third distraction, the "good thought." You've cooked up the plot for the great American novel. You've figured out what to say to that annoying co-worker. You have a business plan, finally. Whatever it may be, it's too good to let go of. But if it is in fact that good, it should be recallable later. And if one wants this practice to work, the deal needs to be to notice and return. Usually to one. Just start over. If you find yourself having all your great ideas in zazen, you may want to set aside a separate time to sit your cushion with a notebook beside you—but don't mistake sitting with a notebook for the spiritual practice of zazen.

AFTER THAT FIRST SITTING at the Zen Center, I was ushered into an interview with a senior priest. Dainin Katagiri Roshi, then called by the title *sensei*, was on duty. I made the bows as I was instructed and sat awkwardly before him.

He asked how long I'd been sitting.

I estimated three, maybe five minutes.

He said, "Good. Keep that mind."

Shunryu Suzuki liked to call and recall people to beginner's mind, which he pointed out has within it many more possibilities than one will find in the mind of an expert. Just start over. As the years passed and I began to take on responsibility for sharing the practice with others, I came to see a few points that I continue to share with beginners about that beginner's mind and what supports it.

Shikantaza

All beings by nature are Buddha,
As ice by nature is water.
Apart from water there is no ice;
Apart from beings, no Buddha.

■ HAKUIN'S "SONG OF ZAZEN" ■

A FEW YEARS after I started sitting regularly I decided I wanted to be a priest. I figured if only I were ordained then all my problems would be solved. The difficulty was that the Zen Center expected people to go through a very long apprenticeship—it could take years. And that didn't seem to make any sense to me.

Besides, just getting to speak to the master seemed beyond me. I attended talks Suzuki Roshi gave; he was always a very small figure very far away speaking in what my friends assured me was English, but to my ear was nearly incomprehensible.

I was brooding over this barrier to getting everything fixed when the Zen master Jiyu Kennett, accompanied by two Western senior disciples, an American and a South African, arrived in San Francisco. She was English, had studied in Japan for a number of years, and was the Dharma successor to a very prominent Japanese Soto Zen master. Kennett Roshi had been authorized to start a Zen center in London and, on her way there from Japan, stopped over at the San Francisco Zen Center to learn how they had successfully adapted Zen training to a Western culture. She hadn't been there a week before she decided it might be better to hang out her shingle in California rather than back home in England. She moved into a flat on Potrero Hill and announced she was receiving visitors.

I was the first person at the door.

I began sitting at her zendo housed in the little flat, and quickly and formally became her student. It was an exhilarating time. We sat a lot. I met in private interviews with her daily. And she gave small and intimate classes on various aspects of the Dharma, beginning to guide me and the rest of a small band of her students to a larger insight into the Zen way, particularly focusing on the insights of both Eihei Dogen, the founding master of Japanese Soto Zen, and Keizan Jokin who transformed Japanese Soto into the largest Zen school in Japan.

Most important for me was that in one of my first interviews with her she told me to stop counting and to practice *shikantaza*, to just sit. She didn't elaborate a lot. She liked the phrase *silent illumination*, a term possibly associated with master Hongzhi in the early twelfth century. It didn't help very much; I found my mind was neither silent, nor illumined. But I persisted.

After I'd had a few intensive months with her, the roshi decided she had to return to England to wind up family affairs; both her parents had died since she left the country. She invited me to move into the temple to cover the rent while she was in England, left the South African disciple in charge of the sangha, and took off for London.

MYOZEN DELPORT, the disciple left in charge, was an Afrikaner who had left her home country to study karate in Japan. She settled in, was very successful in her studies, and at the same time became deeply involved in Zen practice. Among her friends was a young man who became infatuated with her. Focused on karate and particularly on Zen practice, she didn't really notice his growing feelings. One day she had a long conversation with him where she spoke about her desire to ordain. The next morning she learned he had hung himself.

Haunted, Myozen sought to throw herself completely into Zen practice. She obtained an introduction to Kennett Roshi, who told me how she'd sat her new student down in the tiny zendo and had her meditate day in and day out. Every once in a while the roshi would come in and violently strike the young woman across the shoulders with a *kyosaku*, a stick made for the purpose of startling, punishing, or encouraging people in meditation halls. Depending on the pronunciation the stick was said to awaken or to warn. In this case it was to drive her forward.

It did; the ghost haunting her quickly moved on to easier pickings while Myozen learned how to help someone "just sit" in a serious way.

When I wasn't working, I was sitting—every morning, every evening, and much of every weekend. And periodically, Myozen would come into the small zendo with her kyosaku and strike me hard across the shoulders.

It drove me forward.

It drove me inward.

It focused everything.

Now, one doesn't need the stick. I'm moderately confident that for me it pushed things along a bit faster than otherwise might have been the case. But really, the deal is pretty simple; all one needs to do is just sit down, shut up, and pay attention.

This is the universal solvent of the heart.

Become as wide as the sky.

Let the whole of what is play across the screen of the mind and heart.

Just notice.

Koan Introspection

YEARS PASSED. I left Kennett Roshi's tutelage. I investigated other disciplines. Eventually I was given permission to lead a study group in the tradition of the Sufi master Inayat Khan and his famous successor the San Francisco–based mystic Samuel Lewis. Jan and I had opened a bookstore in Guerneville on the Russian River some sixty miles or so north of San Francisco. On Thursday evenings I led the Sufi group in the store. Nothing came of it.

But at the same time, after a hiatus of several years I had resumed a regular Zen sitting practice. One thing about sitting Zen that is probably true about any practice of this sort is how helpful it is to sit with others. So weekday mornings I threw open the doors of the bookstore to anyone who wanted to sit in the Zen style.

Among those who came was Jim Wilson. Jim had been a student of the Korean Zen master Seung Sahn. He had been ordained a monk and for some years served as abbot of the Kwan Um School's center in New York City. At some point Jim went to his teacher and said that he had come to admit to himself that he had ordained in a celibate order as a way to avoid facing his homosexuality. His teacher asked him simply to be discreet. Jim did not find this helpful, so he disrobed and began a journey that would lead him to find a loving partner and to live out on the Russian River. Now all he wanted was a group to sit with. As I said, it feels helpful to sit with others.

What intrigued me about Jim's school of Zen was that they practiced with koans. Koan derives from the Chinese *gongan* and is usually translated as "public case," as in a legal document. While a practice of silence and presence is common in one way or another to all religions and intuited as valuable by many of no religion, koan practice is unique to the Zen schools.

No one knows how they emerged, although one delightful suggestion by a scholar of such things was that they started as an adaptation of a Taoist drinking game. I rather like that idea. What I knew was that koans are questions created out of stories of encounters between Zen masters or masters and students, or out of bits of fables or parts of poems. These questions are said, in the Zen tradition, not to be meaningless but rather to point one somewhere. And I was curious as to where.

I asked Jim to give me a koan. He demurred. While he had been a very senior student he had not been authorized to teach with koans. I asked, a bit manipulatively, I admit, "Don't you want a group to sit with?" I guess I really, really wanted to try koans.

He relented and asked me what I would later learn was part of a koan. He said, "All things return to one." Then he asked, "To what does the one return?"

We were sitting in the front part of my bookstore, the door wide open. I looked at the spines of the books lining the walls, a cascade of color and print. I glanced out the window at the light and tops of trees and buildings. I could hear people talking as they walked along the street below. And the smell, I could smell the country fragrances mixed with gasoline vapors the breeze carried into that room.

And I knew the response.

And I told him.

Later I would learn this was case 45 in the Blue Cliff Record, an early twelfth-century Chinese anthology of koans: A student of the way asks Master Zhaozhou, "All things return to one. To what does the one return?" To which the venerable gave his own answer, "When I was living in Qingzhou I sewed a robe. It weighed seven pounds."

This is no non sequitur, but actually a very honest and straightforward response.

Each of us needs to find where that one returns. In fact everything depends upon it. Whether we know it or not, whether we use this system of introspection or not, the joy and purpose of our lives depends upon our finding the answer to the question.

I would enrich my sitting with these questions for the next year, one after another, investigating the great matter of self and other, of the one and the many, of hurt and loss and finding. While never formally my teacher, Jim certainly was one of my most important teachers. I remain endlessly grateful.

I had found my heart practice.

Listening for the Sound of the Single Hand

■ HOW TO LET A KOAN WORK ON YOU ■

IN CHINA AND KOREA the primary form of koan engagement is through a *huatou* (Chinese; *wato* in Japanese), which literally means "word head." It is seen as the essential point of a koan; the distillation of what might be a larger presentation. In the original practice a student was given one single koan, which was seen as being useful for a lifetime. Occasionally, for various reasons, a practitioner would take on a second or, even more rarely, a third case. But the heart of this was found in fully throwing oneself into one koan. This koan became a touchstone of one's practice.

In Japan and the Japanese-derived koan lineages in the West, koan introspection has taken on a new dimension. By the eighteenth century, various Japanese Rinzai-school Zen teachers began introducing koan "curricula." These were programs of koan study through which a student might "pass" during the course of many years. While there is some dispute over who actually developed this system, it is usually believed to have culminated in the work of the great eighteenth-century master Hakuin Ekaku and his principal students and their students—or, at least, in the work of teachers who followed them. This program is used within Japanese Rinzai to this day. A variation on it is the source of the modern system used in some Soto schools: the so-called Harada-Yasutani curriculum. It is this later practice that has become the heart of my own spiritual life.

Koan study, koan introspection, begins with a step reminiscent of that original way in. The beginning student is given a "breakthrough" koan, a case specifically meant to elicit an initial experience of nonduality. The Japanese term for this koan is *shokan*, or "first barrier." A student might spend years struggling with it, although occasionally someone passes through the breakthrough koan quickly. One never knows.

Most commonly this breakthrough koan is Zhaozhou's "Mu." The set up is simplicity itself. A student of the way comes to Zhaozhou and asks, "Does a dog have buddha nature?" Zhaozhou replies, "Mu." *Mu* means *no*.

Now, there is a lot buried within this exchange. The conversation that becomes this koan takes place near the beginning of the ninth century. In China in that time a dog was vermin. So, does a rat have buddha nature? Does the AIDS virus have buddha nature? And we can assume the student is an old hand and knows the "doctrinally correct" answer: of course a dog has buddha nature. Or, more correctly a dog is a part of buddha nature. Or more precisely still, dogs and buddha nature are one thing.

We can also assume we have no monopoly on low self-esteem. The student is asking about herself, about himself: Do I have buddha nature?

No is an invitation.

In this practice, everything is thrown away except that single sound: Mu.

Did I mention how, of necessity, a student of koans is given insufficient instructions? So there won't be a lot more. One might be advised to "become Mu." One might be asked to mentally wash that Mu through everything one encounters. One might be asked if there is anything that is not Mu.

And then the teacher waits.

Of course, this is a human discipline. And it is subject to misuse, to abuse, to simple misunderstanding. The amount of nonsense written about enlightenment, about awakening, in Zen fills libraries. Maybe your library? Be careful, being able to separate wheat from chaff can take years.

Fortunately we don't have to; here, we're invited to let it go.

MU ISN'T THE ONLY POSSIBLE QUESTION that works as a breakthrough koan. "What was your face before your parents were born?" is another. "Stop the sound of distant temple bell" can work quite nicely. But, here I find myself thinking of what probably is the most widely known koan outside of the Zen tradition.

Master Hakuin asks it. We've all heard the sound of two hands clapping. What is the sound of the single hand?

The oldest reference I can find to that single hand is collected in the *Biyanlu*, the Blue Cliff Record. In a commentary on the eighteenth case, "The National Teacher's Seamless Tomb," written perhaps a hundred years before it was collected into the anthology, the master Xuedou Zhongxian says, "The single palm of the hand does not make a sound in vain."

But it is the eighteenth-century Japanese master Hakuin Ekaku who turns it into the koan most of us have heard as "What is the sound of one hand clapping?" For many it is a nonsense statement. Or a conundrum similar to that question "If a tree falls in the forest, and there is no one to hear it, is there a sound?" People here in the West have played with it over the years. A couple of years ago I was watching an episode of *The Simpsons* where Bart gives Lisa his "understanding" of the case by flapping his fingers onto the palm of his hand, producing a faint clapping sound. Which is actually not such a bad response; it shows the playfulness that koans often require.

But this is very serious play. Koans are actually about life and death—our lives, our deaths—in the most intimate sense about who we are, you and I, about our true home, about what it is to be human and present to what is, all that is. Within that playful question about the sound of a single hand is a pointing to our own encounter with what some call the nondual, a profound step away from clinging to either self or other. In the terminology of Zen the question is an invitation into the great matter.

The actual practice takes many forms—but whatever the form, we are asked to throw ourselves into the great matter wholeheartedly. And so we do, we work at it. Without clear direction we may try our hand at any number of things. At some point we may try critical analysis; at another point, it may become a mantra—chanted, breathed, whispered, yelled. And each time we think we gain some insight, some intimation of what it might mean, we take it into the interview room where, most probably, our teacher will reject our response.

And it does require a teacher. This is a dialogistic discipline. We dig deep, we find, and we present our treasure to someone who can discern fool's gold from the truly precious metal. But, and this is important, the teacher doesn't give us our treasure. She only tests the qualities of what we've found.

He only pushes us to find the real deal. But that real deal, our awakening, is always our own.

My own teacher once told me that awakening comes to us as an accident; and I tell my own students this today. There is no obvious causal relationship between nondual insight and anything we might do or not do. But, he adds, if awakening is an accident, certain practices can help us become accident-prone. Koan practice is particularly effective at this.

If we open ourselves to this great adventure—with due diligence along with our doubt, faith, and energy—eventually it will happen. That bus hits us and everything changes, the world becomes something new and precious. Or perhaps the bus just grazes us as it passes by. But even that graze is valuable. This is the point of most koans. They give us an opportunity to break out of what we thought the world had been all about for us and encounter it anew.

When one has demonstrated insight into the basic matter, the teacher trained in koan introspection may go on to ask "checking questions," which reveal how nuanced our insight is. In the case of a breakthrough koan, there might be dozens or even a hundred checking questions. As we move through the breakthrough koan into other cases, there are usually several checking questions for each case beyond the central point.

So, if one has demonstrated the classic response to the single hand, one may then be asked, "They say when you hear the sound of the single hand you become Buddha. How do you become Buddha?" Or, "Show me the sound of the single hand before your parents were born." Or, "What happens to the single hand when you die?" There are dozens of such questions. More.

Now, there are a few books to be found that purport to

give "answers" to koans. Occasionally, for reasons that completely elude me, people will take another student's answers and present them to their teacher in the interview room—as if some formal or official "passing" of a koan were somehow the important thing, and not our own liberation from our own suffering. It doesn't take too many checking questions to reveal the true quality of a student's insight.

But, really, what's the point in that? It isn't about collecting answers or getting badges, or titles. This is about our hurt and loss, our longing, and our finding. To engage with it honestly, to its best possible purpose, Zen practice requires three things, whether using koans or not: great doubt, great faith, and great determination, points first articulated by the Linji master Gaofeng Yuanmiao.

First, great doubt. It shouldn't be confused with skeptical doubt, as important and powerful as skeptical doubt may be. This is a spiritual call to question authority, and when we start looking into how we engage with the world, it quickly becomes obvious that the highest authority in our lives is the one inside our skulls. It tells us all sorts of things, sometimes in a whisper, sometimes shouted. We're the greatest. Or, just as popular, we're the worst. This authority tells us all sorts of things. And it is a liar. Turning doubt on ourselves, questioning anything we think, we strive to manifest the truth within that bumper sticker "DON'T BELIEVE EVERYTHING YOU THINK." Although the invitation here is even more radical: don't believe anything you think.

Great faith is often discovered within great doubt. It doesn't take much faith to begin a spiritual practice like Zen—for which I'm grateful, because faith doesn't come naturally to me. All one really needs to begin is the feeling that something positive might come out of the discipline. I know that's about all I had when I began. Yes, it is a belief, but of a relatively minor sort. And, if you're willing to suspend disbelief to this limit, it's enough.

Quickly, however, if we take on the discipline and open our hearts and minds into the practice, we find various intimations that enlarge our sense of confidence in this project: our growing faith. This evolving faith becomes Great Faith: our growing openness to what is, and our growing confidence in what we encounter as really being of use on the way. Great faith starts as curiosity and blossoms into a dynamic engagement, a dance of the soul.

In koan introspection, doubt and faith travel together. Each informs the other. It is our relentless presence with doubt and faith that takes us to the gate of nondual insight. Indeed both the path to the gate and the gate itself are discovered within that relentlessness, that willingness to not turn away. This relentlessness is that great determination, which could be thought of as great energy or perhaps great courage.

From an instrumentalist view of koan introspection, words like *Mu* or phrases like "What is the sound of the single hand?" or "What is your original face from before your parents were born?" are often mistakenly assumed to be meaningless. It is assumed that the "point" of such koans is to simply startle the discursive mind into some kind of transrational state. But this understanding of koans simply posits a new dualism: a lower discursive consciousness and a higher nondiscursive state. This is not what koan introspection is about.

Rather, as we push through any koan—experiencing great doubt, great faith, and great determination—we find the exact identity between our ordinary consciousness and fundamental openness. Nondual reality includes subject and object, each itself and freely transposing with the other; first this, now that—sometimes one drops away, sometimes the other, sometimes both drop away, sometimes one emerges from the other, sometimes both emerge together—but we rest nowhere. Resting nowhere and moving fluidly among these perspectives is the true practice of koan introspection—helping us on our way.

Some of What Zen Practice Is, A Little of What It Isn't

WANDERING AROUND the Buddhist blogosphere I ran across a story that purports to be out of the Zen tradition. Frankly, I've never encountered it before and am rather suspicious about its origins. The message it contains is one that I've found commonly held to be "Zen," mainly from people who've never actually studied Zen in the sense of taking Zen on as a spiritual discipline, finding a regular practice and connecting with a teacher.

It goes somewhat like this. A senior student decides it is time for him to be acknowledged as a master of the Zen way and goes to his teacher to discuss the matter. It is raining so the student has an umbrella. When he comes to the teacher's cottage, before entering he sets the umbrella down outside the door and, as this is Japan, or at least a Zen story, he takes off his shoes and sets them down next to the umbrella. Once inside, he tells his teacher that it is now time for him to be acknowledged as a teacher in his own right. In response the teacher asks whether he used an umbrella on his walk to the cottage. The student replies yes. The teacher asks on what side of the umbrella the student left his shoes. The student cannot reply, is given a lecture about mindfulness, then sent back to the meditation hall.

Now, noticing each moment and remembering what one has done are laudable things. That noticing is the germ of the Zen discipline. But thinking Zen is about attending and remembering is missing the point by, oh let's say, by a mile. The way of awakening is about opening the mind and heart. Being here fully as we are, forgetfulness and all.

"Mindfulness" is just an expression: be mindful of where you've put the umbrella. In an important way, saying "forgetting" could be just as useful: the umbrella was part of the last moment, completely gone—forget it, why harp on the past? Although then we'd have all sorts of Zen students proudly proclaiming how they forgot their umbrella...

The problem here is rather like the "debate" between advocates of self-power and other-power. Most religions are all about other-power. God in Western religions, Amida Buddha in the Pure Land. The rhetoric of Zen, however, is filled mainly with self-power allusions. One is told to put one's concentration to the matter and to not turn away, not even if it costs you your life. And people do just that, with verve and gusto. I admire those who throw themselves into the matter with everything they've got. But it really is a bit more complicated. Often the way is found when one finally, finally, lets go of the last desperate idea of what "it" is supposed to "mean." One surrenders. And it turns out the great joke of self-power and other-power is that there is no debate.

Mohammed is said to have told us that if one of us is willing to advance one step toward God, God will run a hundred steps toward us. If we don't get trapped in that koanic word *God* we can get a real pointer on the way for us.

Take some initiative. And then be ready to be surprised, by joy, by freedom, by the whole mess.

And here's another pointer: Noticing the umbrella is a good thing. Notice it. Then when you don't need it, put it down.

Don't worry about remembering.

Don't worry about forgetting.

Rain or shine, with your teacher or alone, it is already here.

Spiritual Directors

NEAR THE BEGINNING of my Zen practice, I'd had a deeply conflicted relationship with a teacher. Jiyu Kennett taught me much of enormous value, but there was also the whiff of cult about her. Several former students, including me, carry deep wounds that resulted from her questionable actions. And yet I had experiences under her guidance that would become the foundation of my spiritual life, and have played out for many years. At bottom I owe her my entire life.

If one chooses to take up with a Zen teacher, there is a better than passing chance that not everything you get will be helpful. In fact if the relationship is real and deep there will almost certainly be a certain kind of failure, betrayal, and hurt. But, here's the hard part, don't get confused between the ordinary, human betrayals and the hurts that do and must call for intervention.

There are lines that should not be crossed and transgressions that must be objected to. Obviously sexual ethics is one area, but this caution is true of so much of our lives. While ethics are indeed situational, those situations can and often do demand we stand up for or against. It is all about being present to the situation, fully. Fortunately, as we bring our lives into harmony with the Tao, with the Way, "right" responses usually will be pretty obvious.

And if a satisfactory response is not found, the students

who were subjected to or witnesses of these crossed lines need to leave. And probably should make public what happened, to warn others. In recent years much has been made of sexual scandals regarding spiritual teachers and particularly Zen teachers. Paying attention to and dealing with sexual misconduct and all other forms of abuse is critical to the maturation of the Dharma come West.

It is complicated. And can be scary. But at the same time there is so much value in finding someone who has walked out into the desert of the heart and who can help us as we launch into that strange and mysterious territory on our own quest—I suggest it is well worth the difficulties, and even the dangers.

And so, as my time with Jim—the man who introduced me to the koan way—began to wind down, I knew I needed a teacher, specifically someone skilled in the koan way. The problem is that there aren't all that many people who are authorized, much less competent, in guiding people in this ancient discipline. But I was determined.

By this time Jan and I had decided to close the bookstore, and begin a process of putting each other through school, a process that would lead her to become a librarian and me a Unitarian Universalist minister. While finishing my undergraduate degree at Sonoma State University I found a job in a downtown Santa Rosa used bookstore.

Of the many teachers I knew of, the one that most captured my imagination was Robert Aitken, an American and one of the first Westerners to receive full Dharma transmission, acknowledgment as a Zen master. Most importantly, he was a master of the koan way and had a long history of involvement in issues of justice, which I felt should be connected to the spiritual life. The major problem was that I lived in California and he lived in Hawaii. I decided to write him a letter describing my spiritual journey and solicited his advice at this juncture in my life. It proved to be a long letter.

I dropped it in a mailbox down the street from the bookstore as I went in to work. Later that day a couple walked in to the store. The woman was elegantly dressed. She wandered into the literature area. The man, about my height, bearded, roughly my age, dressed casually, asked if we had anything interesting by way of Orientalia. I replied, "Why yes, we have a delightful little book by Lafcadio Hearn, a Japanese ghost story with hand-colored plates." He asked to look at it. We went over to the locked bookcase, I opened it and handed him the book. It was beautiful. He said, "I'll take it."

I was curious and asked if he was a collector. He replied, no, he was not, and told me he was looking for a gift for his teacher. I asked, "Teacher of what?" He replied, "Zen." His name was John Tarrant, and he was Robert Aitken's first Dharma successor.

John Tarrant was born in Tasmania, and raised in a house without indoor plumbing. He won a scholarship to the National University, where he majored in psychology and literature. At some point he discovered Buddhism and, following his own karmic path, ended up in Hawaii where he studied with Aitken Roshi. I quickly saw just how good he was with koans. Even now, decades later and with a lot of experience under my belt, I can't think of anyone more skillful in guiding that particular discipline.

But I hesitated. I wasn't sure if I wanted a formal relationship with this man. John was clearly smart and knew his way around a koan. But I felt there was something a bit reckless about him, which manifested in part as big-time charisma. And, truthfully, it didn't help that he was also a year younger than me.

Then, out of the blue, I learned that Seung Sahn was going to lead a seven-day retreat in Berkeley. As it was his style of koan that was my first experience of the discipline, I was excited at the chance to meet and practice with the master. I registered and attended. It was great. I liked the Korean style, which was more informal, although just as rigorous in the things that mattered. And in particular I liked Master Seung Sahn. He had a ready laugh, and was fierce in pushing us to our own encounter with the great matter.

But they served kimchee with breakfast. I took that as a symbol for all that is wrong with Zen come West.

Don't get me wrong; I like kimchee, a pickled cabbage that can be quite spicy, and always tasty. But there was just no blessed reason that a meditation retreat that had exactly two Korean nationals out of about thirty people attending, and one of them part time, should make kimchee part of everyone's breakfast meal. Now the dance between the cultural inheritance that fostered the Dharma and the culture to which it is transplanted is complex, and it is always hard to say what's too much. But this just didn't work for me, not at that time in my life.

And even worse was how many of the participants, including quite senior students, mimicked Master Seung Sahn's broken English. One does not need to sound like Master Yoda to be wise. I felt this too much by half. Again, at least at this time in my life and where I needed my own practice to find itself.

When the retreat ended, I had already made an appointment to meet John at the cheap Chinese restaurant down the block from the bookstore where we regularly ate and talked. We sat together and I gave him a small box of incense, the formal way one becomes a student in the tradition.

I've had my regrets along the way. I'm moderately confident he has, as well. John's a larger-than-life figure who cares little for institutions and rules, and this has come home on occasion. He is often seen as one of the bad boys of Western Zen.

And he proved to be exactly the teacher I needed.

John was able to push me on my own personal, truly intimate way into the depths of who I really am. Within my relationship with him as a Zen student he had absolutely no judgments about me as a person—an amazing capacity, although it presents its own difficulties. Accordingly, I never really knew whether he really liked me or not. However, I learned relatively quickly that this didn't matter. All he wanted from me was for me to see into the great matter and out of that to find my own way. And thanks to him I did. I owe him endless bows.

And to his teacher.

And to his teacher.

All the way...

What to Look for When Looking for a Zen Teacher

BEFORE SEEKING OUT a teacher in the Zen tradition, it would be wise to read a little about all the traditions you sense might help you. If, after a period of reading and questioning, you think Zen might be the path for you, then continuing to read about Zen is important.

But more important, if the Zen path sounds right for you, I would suggest you start by taking up the practice of Zen meditation pretty much right now. You can get the basics out of many good books: John Daishin Buksbazen's *Zen Meditation in Plain English* would be a very good way to start, as would Robert Aitken's *Taking the Path of Zen*. A visit to a local Zen group of any flavor can provide some hands-on instruction that can clarify most beginning questions.

You don't have to sign up for anything other than an introductory class, nor, I strongly suggest, should you. Just check things out. If you like the group, perhaps keep going from time to time. But do begin to sit at home regularly. Cultivate a discipline. If after a reasonable amount of time, perhaps six months or so, maybe a year, the practice doesn't feel right, you really don't need to look for a Zen teacher. After all, any real Zen teacher is going to return you over and over again to the practice. If you don't feel a connection to zazen, you can probably find another practice tradition that will be more fruitful.

If, on the other hand, Zen continues to seem to be the best way of addressing the concerns that propel you on the spiritual path, then—and really only then—should you begin to look for a teacher in earnest. At that point, it becomes important for you to sort through the hundreds of teachers and dozens of communities to find one that fits you well. If this book helps with nothing else, I hope it shows how different Zen communities might be, how one could be completely wrong for you and another could be just what you need.

I cannot recommend a seeker join any community led by Zen teachers who will not say who taught them and who gave them permission to teach. Though such people may perhaps be wise beings, the problems that can hide in the shadows of such a stance are just too numerous and too potentially dangerous. If you're in doubt whether a teacher is what she or he says, and you're in America or Canada, you can look at the website of the American Zen Teachers Association (www.americanzenteachers.org). While not a complete list of all authentic Zen teachers in America, it is a list of a large majority of them. If a prospective teacher (or her or his teacher) is not on the list, chances are that person is significantly outside the mainstream of Zen.

Next, consider the possibilities within the authentic Zen paths. Do your inclinations take you toward monastic practice? Are you attracted to the priestly traditions? Or perhaps a lay-led community feels best. Hopefully this book has helped to show what those distinctions mean. Clarifying this can really help in finding the right teacher and the right community.

That said, at the beginning it's hard to know what will

be best in your particular situation. Here trusting one's instincts isn't a bad thing, particularly if you're also open to proving yourself wrong and have cultivated some sense of humility as you begin to explore unknown territory.

Ask people you respect who have walked a spiritual path for some time whom they might recommend—just like you might if you were looking for a good doctor. Also: most Zen groups now have websites. Read them. And visit. Those things alone will reveal a great deal both about the teacher and the community. Is it all about the teacher, or is there more to it? I recommend you do this with several communities. Since you're already maintaining a practice, there's no rush to sign on with a teacher. Take your time. Choose carefully.

But please be very clear about this: Zen teachers are not gurus. They—we—are not perfect masters. A real Zen teacher is completely, unambiguously, human with a full complement of challenges and shortcomings. Every teacher has flaws. The task is not to find a perfect teacher (you can't) but to find one who, warts and all, can be a good-enough guide on the Zen path. You need to be ready to be surprised.

It's probably not wise to make a decision about the right teacher based mostly on witnessing their public persona. It's really impossible to make a useful judgment of a possible teacher by how they give a Dharma talk, what they say in one magazine interview, or even what they write in a book.

I suggest a different approach: when visiting a teacher or a center, examine the teacher's students. Are they simply clones-in-training of the teacher? This is probably not a good thing—after all, Zen is about becoming more fully yourself, not becoming more like your teacher. On the other hand, do the students who've been around a while seem to be people you like, and might like to be with? Can you recognize the values they advocate? Are they independent and engaged in the world? Can they joke about themselves? And, importantly, can they joke about their institution and teacher? And more important still: Do they seem to be genuinely on a path that is freeing them from their suffering?

This step of evaluating the community is an important one and one I strongly urge you not to skip. After all, the community, the sangha is as much the teacher as the person with the title. Often, actually, the community is even more the teacher than the person with the title.

Only Don't Know

IN THE ZEN TRADITION the primary practice is often described as the "unborn mind," "beginner's mind," or, in what I often find to be the most useful pointer, "not knowing." In case 20 of the koan anthology called the *Congronglu*, the Book of Equanimity, we get a sense of how it is encountered.

The monk Fayan visited Master Dizang, who asked the young student of the way, "Where have you come from?" Fayan replied, "I wander from here to there on my pilgrimage." The master asked, "What is the point of your pilgrimage?" Fayan answered, "I don't know." Master Dizang replied, "Not knowing is most intimate."

The modern Buddhist critic Stephen Batchelor writes of how Thomas Huxley coined the term *agnostic* to describe the path of his own spiritual inquiry. While I'm less enthusiastic about some aspects of Batchelor's work, we'll return to that later; I remain grateful for the pointer to this rich word *agnostic* and to the man who coined it. *Agnostic* means "without knowledge," or "not knowing"—however, not in the sense we commonly find today of "I don't know and I don't particularly care."

Rather, Huxley's agnosticism had a lot of heart about it; he followed this way with great passion. For Huxley agnosticism was a discipline, as compelling as a creed. Well, maybe not creed, because Huxley wasn't seeking pat answers. For him agnosticism was first and foremost a method. The method he had in mind is broadly the same as that which underpins scientific inquiry. And for him this method led to a naturalistic, and what we might call today a "humanistic" spirituality.

For me this approach is immensely important. I'm a person of little faith: I'm not willing to accept something just because someone has said it is so, even someone I admire enormously, even the Buddha. If something claims objective reality, it is testable. If it fails the test, well... Also, my own tumble into the way of awakening has been all about not knowing, or as Master Seung Sahn says, "only don't know." Only don't know. Not-knowing. That little shift breaks the world open. And it is this not-knowing mind that I have found opening my heart and the way. It is the place where science and religion meet, where the creative spirit births, where all possibilities emerge.

Not-knowing allows us to see things in new light, to discern much about the human heart. Huxley's rigorous observations within the spirit of not-knowing led to some basic principles that can inform us, and take us deep into the ways of wisdom. And for me it has been a great relief to discover I don't have to accept the unlikely to walk the Way.

I'm also very much aware I can be wrong, in my views, opinions, and beliefs about practice. After all, reality so often shows me that I am flat out wrong. And the claims of generations of spiritual practitioners cannot simply be dismissed.

A fairly obvious area is the dichotomy between material and spiritual. And this is a criticism that cuts both the spiritual and the materialist. In an important way, I simply don't understand what this division is supposed to mean in a universe where everything is at once separate and one. We're completely material. We're completely spiritual. Now this, now that. One thing. To find this we open ourselves wide— we open into not-knowing.

And there are many other areas where a genuine sense of not knowing opens new angles of investigation. For instance, whether God exists was not a primary concern to Huxley, although he saw no reason to postulate a deity. Huxley's real challenge for most of us cut much closer to the bone. He challenged how we see ourselves. He was adamant that *human beings* did not exist outside the flow of events and their intimate interrelatedness.

Huxley wrote, "In the whole universe there is nothing permanent, no eternal substance either of mind or of matter." He felt any idea of an abiding self, an eternal individual "personality is a metaphysical fancy; and in very truth not only we, but all things in the worlds without end of the cosmic phantasmagoria, are such stuff as dreams are made of." Understanding this viscerally becomes a key to authentic wisdom.

The late Unitarian Universalist theologian Forrest Church observed that the work of religion flows out of our knowledge that we are alive and that we are going to die. I would add that spirituality addresses the hurt, fear, and anxiety that seems to haunt the human condition and, to my mind, arises out of a fundamental cognitive error: that we are isolated beings.

Certainly, as I look at myself honestly, relentlessly, in the spirit of not-knowing, frankly I find it impossible to discern any part of me that isn't formed by conditions ranging from my genetic makeup to my ongoing encounters with events and people. I am *this* because of *that*. And the "that" that makes "this" changes in a heartbeat—who I am changes, sometimes slightly, sometimes dramatically, with the very next addition of experience.

As I experience it all, it seems we are all part of a great current flowing from some unknown source to some unknown end, like a river on its way to an ocean. All we know with anything even approaching certainty is this moment itself. And we need to notice what we find here.

To work the image a bit, here is the water, of course, rushing on. But there are many other things, as well. Bits of this and that, sticks and pebbles, whatever. Sometimes a bit of brush gets caught toward the edge of the river, and various things collect together in a swirl. This little eddy of stuff is me. Another is you. Just as real as can be. And just as temporary. For me a swirling eddy of Jamesishness. Then, somewhere along the line something will happen and the eddy of stuff that is James will disappear, but the current will continue rushing on, taking new shapes, new forms, each for a moment, before again resuming that great flow from dark to dark.

There are all sorts of reasons why we see ourselves as separate from each other. To me it seems obvious it is an unfortunate side effect of our amazing ability to divide the universe, to find the information that allows us to survive. And there certainly is a truth that in any given moment we are in fact separate. You are you and I am I, at least in the moment. And at the very same time there is a larger sense in which we are totally wrapped up together in a very real web of mutuality. The intuition of the spiritual enterprise is that with discarding or collapsing we can reconcile these apparent contradictions: our separateness in the moment, and our essential connectedness. This is sometimes called the "nondual perspective."

Through his commitment to not-knowing, Huxley, it certainly seems, found the nondual perspective. While he, like the Buddha, was writing before the discovery of genes, he got the principle that we are all moments in the great rush of time and space, verbs rather than nouns, notes in a symphony.

The spiritual enterprise, as I see it, is to find how this is in fact our own truth, yours and mine. And it is discovered when we open our hearts and minds, as we embrace a way of deep agnosticism, of truly not knowing. Deep agnosticism, not turning away, remaining present, heals many wounds.

Susan Blackmore in her lovely book *Consciousness: An Introduction* relates a story that shows what the realization of nonduality might look like. She gives the example of John Wren-Lewis, a sixty-year-old physics professor. While traveling in Thailand he was poisoned by a thief. Awakening from the drug-induced coma, he was aware of a persistent experience of a "dazzling darkness." Out of this he found he now lived with a continuing experience, in which everything "seemed perfectly right and as it should be." He found his life an expression of nonduality.

I'm very taken that Blackmore didn't choose an example from the traditional spiritual literature. This wasn't a thirty-year practitioner of an austere spiritual discipline. This was someone drugged and robbed. This experience is accessible to all of us because it is a natural part of how our brains naturally work. Meditation and other disciplines help, a lot. But in the last analysis all we need do is let go of our certainties. I don't know why we are able to do this. But I do know that we can—that I've experienced. As have endless others.

By the way, some sense of this experience never abandoned Wren-Lewis for the rest of his life. In his own words Wren-Lewis described the place of not-knowing: "I feel as if the back of my head has been sawn off so that it is no longer the sixty-year-old John who looks out at the world, but the shining dark infinite void that in some extraordinary way is also 'I.'"

This is where not knowing takes us, each following our own trajectory, each with our own moments, and all joined. For me I found it sitting in a Buddhist monastery, eating a thin cabbage soup. For you, perhaps playing with a child. For another, perhaps listening to Mozart. Another, perhaps just noticing that it is possible for this moment only to not have that drink. For another, well, who knows? The secret is not knowing.

Only don't know. Deep agnosticism.

As the master Dizang said, "Not knowing is most intimate."

I suggest a deep agnosticism; truly engaging not-knowing is the universal solvent. It will release us from our hurt and fears by showing us, not in some abstract cognitive therapy sort of way, but in the deepest, most visceral way, who we really are.

Open, wide as the sky. And at the very same time intimate, more intimate than any word can ever convey. And the way to this wisdom is simple.

Just don't know.

Only don't know.

That's all it takes.

PART III

Talking the Talk, Walking the Walk

They show that what the law requires is written on
their hearts, to which their own conscience also
bears witness; and their conflicting thoughts will
accuse or perhaps excuse them.

■ ROMANS 2:15 ■

Putting It Together

THE REALITY of our lives may be informed by various forms of meditation. I know for me just how important zazen and koan introspection have been. They opened vast vistas. And those vistas themselves, that discovery we are not only precious and unique as individuals, but that we take our existence from and within the world itself, that we are one and many, is the high road of wisdom.

And then we must throw ourselves into the lived world. If one looks at the Buddha's original Eightfold Path, it could be broken into three broad categories. One is meditation. Another is that nondual insight. And the third has to do with how we order our lives, how we live in this world that is now one, now separate, where our intentions and our actions birth our lives.

In the chapters in this section I offer some reflections on how we engage, how we live in ways that are graceful and authentic.

FIRST, IT'S ALL ABOUT THE MIND. Right at the beginning it is critical to understand our minds. This is the meeting place of the individual and the world, it is here we find our lives. And it turns that out simply trying to understand what one's mind is and is for can be complicated. There are all sorts of ways people misunderstand the mind. Have you ever been mugged and then had a friend ask you why you wanted that to happen? A friend of mine was, and a mutual friend did. The premise within this exchange is that we are in control of what happens to us and that if we're right with the universe, everything we want will be ours.

And, so, if we have cancer, we wanted it. If a child is born into a war and starves to death. If you're raped, if you're born into poverty, if you have a spouse that beats you; if you're rich, if you have everything handed to you on a golden platter, if you live to be a hundred and two—all your choice.

This is not true.

If it were true, then, well, however hard or wonderful it is, we would have to deal with that hard truth. I'm very much up for hard truths. So long as they're true. But in this case, it's not. Rather, it reflects a profound misunderstanding of how the universe and our human minds work.

Let me offer a contrary view, a tad more consonant with the evidence at hand.

The universe is very big. It consists of many, many different things going on, each influencing other things. At some point everything is connected with everything. In a last-analysis sort of way, we are all connected. And, so, what we think, what we feel, what we say, and what we do are parts of that great mix of motions that lead to other motions.

But here's the sad news: You are not the center of the universe. Nor am I. At least not in any way having to do with our egos. After all, egos too are simply constructs caused by many factors, and in existence only for the briefest moment in time, existing until the factors shift. Here's a hard truth: The universe doesn't give a flying fig that you want to be rich, or healthy, or anything in particular.

Don't get me wrong—what happens inside your skull is important; and adjusting your attitude can certainly have salutary effects. But while it is helpful, sometimes mightily helpful, in the last analysis adjusting attitudes doesn't cure diseases—to say nothing of old age and death. And for those who insist otherwise and scurry about with stories of this or that miraculous cure: anecdote doesn't replace science. If you want to claim some action causes something in the real world, don't look for a feel-good book, or a kindly looking physician with a smooth pitch; find the studies that prove it.

Again, adjusting your attitude has power. There is some evidence attitudes can enhance healing processes, and certainly can contribute to contentment. More important, perhaps, adjusting your attitude can inspire you to get off your duff and do things. And that's a miracle, of sorts. But don't confuse the matter. You cannot make yourself a money magnet. You cannot imagine away cancer. And no matter what you think, you will die.

And this is the important point: this "adjust your attitude and cure cancer" is the near enemy of something profound. It is the "near enemy" because it looks like the real deal, but if you settle for it, you miss that great treasure. Look to wake up. Open your heart. Open your mind. Look for that which will actually help you to heal your heart and to be fully here in this world. And be open to the fact that this healing is nothing so small as curing cancer.

If we actually wake up to who we are, we will discover a great and compelling intimacy. Then we find where the phrase "the mind of God" is meaningful. With our own hearts, our own environment, our own lives.

The call is to tumble into the stream, to learn the current, to flow toward the great ocean. And, I've noticed, as we discover this truth, as we tumble into the Way, we are changed. Our hearts become larger. We care more, and our actions can become the work of God, even if we're only tending a tiny corner of the vineyard.

That's what the ancient teachings are really pointing to.

Karma, Rebirth, & Finding a Real Life

Sow a thought and you reap an action
Sow an action and you reap a habit
Sow a habit and you reap a character
Sow a character and you reap a destiny

■ WESTERN FOLK APHORISM ■

JOHN BLOFELD was a singular Buddhist figure of the twentieth century whose books provided a window on Buddhist practice when there were few to find in the English language. So it probably was considered a coup when he agreed to write the introduction to Stephen Batchelor's 1983 book, *Alone with Others: An Existential Approach to Buddhism.* No doubt Blofeld thought the young monk worth reading; he described the book as "magnificent" and "inspiring." He added how he hoped Batchelor would some day also explore the core doctrines of karma and rebirth.

Fourteen years later, a decade after Blofeld's death, Batchelor published his controversial broadside *Buddhism without Beliefs.* We will never know what the old Buddhist scholar and practitioner would have thought of this analysis, which was a radical departure from traditional expositions of the Buddha's Way, but it's unlikely he would have been happy about it. In this latter book Batchelor asserts:

The idea of rebirth is meaningful in religious Buddhism only insofar as it provides a vehicle for the key Indian metaphysical doctrine of actions and their results known as "karma." While the Buddha accepted the idea of karma as he accepted that of rebirth, when questioned on the issue he tended to emphasize its psychological rather than its cosmological implications.

To me this is retrojection—Batchelor is claiming his contemporary view was the Buddha's as well, which I find unlikely. But what is significant about this passage, aside from its central rejection of more traditional Buddhist beliefs, is that Batchelor eloquently articulates one of the constellation of perspectives that mark a contemporary embrace of the Buddha's teachings. Here our underlying Western rational and humanistic perspectives encounter the Dharma: challenging it, being challenged by it, and ultimately synthesizing with it.

There does appear to be a new Buddhism emerging. It is a Buddhism clearly continuous with its source and, at the same time, quite different from traditional Asian Buddhism. It includes "atheistic" Buddhists such as Stephen Batchelor, as he seems to prefer to call himself these days; more psychologically oriented non-Buddhist Buddhist practitioners such as Toni Packer and Susan Blackmore; scientists and particularly psychologists or neuroscientists who are also immersed in Buddhism, such as Jon Kabat-Zinn, Barry Magid, and James Austin; folk like myself who see themselves as Buddhists but engage the faith openly and are gratefully informed and cautioned by the Western traditions of rational inquiry and social engagement; and, of course, various combinations thereof.

Looking closely, we can't ignore the fact that assumptions held by many Western Buddhists, maybe even the majority, differ—sometimes subtly, sometimes radically—from those held by what for lack of a better term I'd call "traditional" Buddhists.

I think many of these shifting assumptions are of great value, and some are central to my understanding of the Dharma—but they are shifts and need to be noticed and noted as such. And this is important. What we don't notice about ourselves is the most dangerous part of who we are. For instance, Western Zen communities, particularly convert Western Buddhist communities, often make the claim that the Zen teacher transmits an ahistorical path: the once and future Way of Awakening, teachings unchanged from the time they came from the mouth of the Buddha himself. This can be profoundly misleading.

It is also seductive for new movements to see themselves as returning to the "pure" traditions and "original" teachers. Donald Lopez observes this in his preface to *A Modern Buddhist Bible: Essential Readings from East and West*. Certainly, many who hold contemporary Buddhist views see themselves—truthfully, *we* see *ourselves*—as returning to the tenets of an original Buddhism.

Perhaps the most appropriate term to describe this emerging and pervasive perspective is "liberal Buddhism." The word *liberal* derives from Latin and means, among other things, "free and generous." Thus liberal Buddhism is a Buddhism that contributes most genuinely to freedom and is most generous in its approach and application.

The doctrines of karma and rebirth are one area with which I find a free and generous engagement to be a necessary component of any movement of Buddhism to the West. Within Buddhist orthodoxy there are a number of views about karma and rebirth and their necessary connections. The historic Buddha's view is probably best described within the twelvefold chain of causation, the doctrine of dependent origination. Ignorance gives rise to mental formations, which give rise to consciousness, which gives rise to names and forms, which give rise to the sense gates, which give rise to contacts, to feelings, to cravings, to clinging, which lead to becoming, which leads to birth. And then the whole thing begins again in a recurring cycle. Much of the Buddha's concern was how to break this chain, this cycle which is profoundly marked by hurt, by suffering.

And Buddhists have reflected on this analysis over the ages. There is a consensus that there is no permanent or abiding self. Rather the self arises out of causes and conditions. But, and this is central to classical Buddhist thought, while there is no permanent or abiding self this also does not mean there is no continuity across time and space. This concurs with what the Buddha seems clearly to have taught where he denied any abiding self, and yet could or did describe his own past lives. Out of this last point the theory of rebirth arises.

In the classical formulations, karma and rebirth are necessarily connected. Our actions—and even more important, our intentions—create the circumstances for a new birth. Even if one can say in some sense this new person is not exactly the previous person, the connections and the responsibility are a thread continuing through time. Again, in the classic Buddhist understanding, a thread that needs cutting.

And over time karma has taken on various additional shades of meaning. Karma in the popular imagination is some sort of cosmic moral law. And in its inexorable movements, all wrongs are righted and all rights are rewarded. It also has become the explanation of preference for many people hoping to explain the ills of the world—including the majority of Buddhists throughout history. For example, one is poor because in a previous life one was extravagant. Here we find explanations for children starving as well as justifications for the current social order being kept in place. This isn't the same as the confusion of ego that I discussed as the near enemy of the awakened mind in the previous section. But for practical purposes, it isn't all that different. Someone is blamed for being who they are. One's current distress is directly connected to choices made in a previous life. If this were true, we would of course have to deal with it. But, I seriously question that it is.

The renowned Tibetan scholar B. Alan Wallace warns how Batchelor and others who take this view are going against the weight of tradition, "Dogen Zenji, founder of the Soto school of Zen…" Wallace notes, "addressed the importance of the teachings on rebirth and karma in his principal anthology, *Treasury of the Eye of the True Dharma (Shobogenzo)*. In his book *Deep Faith in Cause and Effect (Jinshin inga)*, he criticizes Zen masters who deny karma, and in *Karma of the Three Times (Sanji go)*, he goes into more detail on this matter."

I take this challenge seriously. As a Soto Zen teacher I am a direct successor to Eihei Dogen, and I respect his memory and am informed by his Dharma. And the same can be said for my relationship to the teachings of Gautama Siddhartha, the Buddha of history, the founder of the way I follow. I hesitate at any challenge to their authority. I take that hesitation seriously.

And Wallace is right, to challenge or deny the traditional teaching of the connections between karma and rebirth is moving away from Buddhist orthodoxy—and some would claim moving away from Buddhism. Yet for many who consider themselves faithful disciples of the way, that classical view just doesn't work. You may count me as one. While the Buddha was a spiritual genius, it seems this model of karma and rebirth is good poetry and has enormous psychological utility, and is a pointer to a truer reality. But I have to assert, drawing on the realities of my experience and the insights of science, that it isn't objectively and literally "true" in the sense we usually use that word.

Here's the hard truth I find I must indeed live with, one that is not only hard but also true: there is no calculating engine driving some great karma machine, nor any cosmic mechanism that focuses the consequences of intentions and actions of one life on to a subsequent life. There have been many serious attempts at finding evidence of post-mortem incarnations—but none stand up to hard analysis. Instead we see that the good and ill of an individual lives on, but not in a new single body—rather, among those who that person touched in life, in the fruit of their actions as they touched the world, and in the world itself.

While all things are connected, endlessly, it appears, the mechanisms are often completely amoral. Wrongs are not righted and in fact are instead often perpetuated over very long periods of time. It really does seem that our condition in life has mostly to do with genes and circumstances that are so complex in their origin that "random" is a very good descriptor. From the perspective of human experience, the universe and each of our circumstances within it *just is*.

But this isn't a "you live, you die, you merely feed the worms" perspective. There is much to be found when we throw ourselves into that *just is*. Among other things a moral perspective does appear. But it does not require our adding extras to the universe such as the karma machine.

Here I offer another view, a liberal Buddhist view. It is "a" view, not "the" view. In fact one can hold both classical views and the one I'm about to offer at the same time; such is the richness of the human mind. But I see ways of understanding both karma and rebirth that align more naturally with the world as we commonly experience it. Here the appeal to the psychological value of karma and rebirth makes a lot of sense, although this is not merely psychological—it is about attuning one's perspectives to the universal, finding the harmonious stance with the cosmos.

From this perspective a simple definition: *Karma* is the observation that everything has causes and everything has consequences; *rebirth* is the observation that I am constantly being created and recreated by each succeeding moment. This more psychological understanding of karma and rebirth can be seen as a liberal Buddhist perspective but it is also the perspective of many who walk the Zen way in the West, many of whom probably do not consider themselves part of the liberal trend in Western Buddhism.

These are important questions because they address the *why* of hurt and loss and the *how* of healing. In theological language this is soteriology, the science or more properly (I feel) art of salvation, of healing. So the art of healing is a call to encounter fully the web of relationships, and to consider how our intimate actions constantly reshape the world and how we ourselves are reborn each moment into this mysterious, lovely, and terrible home.

As we best understand the Buddha's message, the karmic cycle of birth and rebirth is itself the expression of the grasping heart, and our salvation is breaking that cycle. Within the liberal vision we still have the hurt of the grasping heart, but the cycles are all found here and now. Speculation about past or future lives seems unnecessary to the project. And since there are simpler explanations for the rise of human consciousness and what happens to it, Occam's Razor suggests it is unnecessary to hold the classical view in order to follow the Buddha Way, particularly as that Way is expressed within the Zen school.

And there is more to a liberal Buddhism than how it engages karma and rebirth and the way we understand suffering, its cause, and its cure. Bhikkhu Bodhi, Western Buddhist monk, renowned English translator of the Buddha's teachings, and critic of the contemporary Buddhist movement, notes three elements marking what I call liberal Buddhism, each creating the conditions most commonly found for Zen practice in the West.

One of these marks is a shift from monastic to lay life as the "principal arena of Buddhist practice." Second, there is an "enhanced position of women" in this newer Buddhism. Third, we also find "the emergence of a grass-roots engaged Buddhism aimed at social and political transformation." And underlying all this is, Bhikkhu Bodhi suggests, a fourth characteristic: a pervasive secularization of the Buddha Way. This often-missed shift is perhaps the most important of all. Let's look at an example of this trend.

Many liberal Buddhists, like other Buddhists, see Buddhist meditation disciplines and Buddhist teachings, in general, as "scientific." But this belief, held by liberals and conservatives alike, is, frankly, untrue. Scientific method requires that there be a possibility of falsification. And experimental science requires replicability: the same practices done the same way should reliably produce the same results. But never, not even in liberal Buddhism, does one hear that if one does the practices and does not achieve liberation, then Buddhism is somehow proven false. Rather, if one does the practices without the promised experiences, most Buddhist teachers will say one has simply not done the practices correctly. This is not science; it is a form of scientism.

The seed of this appeal to science for justification is twofold. What allows this claim to be made is that Buddhism is at heart profoundly empirical. Buddhist insight is based on the experiences of many people over many centuries. Indeed, Buddhist philosophies and psychologies all flow from introspection and examination of those experiences. And empiricism, while not science, is the mother of science. Thus we can see how easily the shift from empirical to scientific might happen.

The second factor driving the appeal to science is the desire of exponents of liberal Buddhism to appear to be up-to-date, current, modern. This impulse had particular appeal in the nineteenth century, when our Buddhists forebears were first asserting their insights as equal to or perhaps better than those offered by Western religions. And it seems as compelling to Buddhists now as it did then.

Appeals to contemporary physics as "proof" of some aspect of Buddhist doctrine is typical of Buddhism, both liberal and conservative. And here, I might add, we find some real shadows: a whole collection of logical fallacies. First among these is the old chestnut, the Appeal to Authority:

the fallacious belief that if a credentialed person says something, it must perforce be true.

There is however a more dangerous effect of unconscious scientism, which is the inclination toward reductionism. This is another great shadow of secularism, and is something liberal Buddhists need to be particularly wary of. Reductionism causes Buddhism to become nothing more than a nostrum for improving one's self-esteem or tennis game, or for getting an edge in business or war. This is not what Buddhism is about, it is not what Zen is about. Nor, frankly, is it about relaxation, calmness, achieving less anxiety, or attenuating depression. While it may indeed have salutary effects on all these things, ultimately it is about something else.

Buddhism is a religion. Although religion with a twist. In some senses Buddhism holds the potential within that popular phrase "spiritual but not religious." While not overly concerned with cosmologies and the workings of gods, at least as it is commonly engaged in the West, it is profoundly concerned with the same questions as all religions: how best to address the facts that we are alive and that we know we will die, that the world is filled with hurts small and great, and that our own hearts are divided. Buddhism is all about salvation, from the Latin *salve*, to heal. It makes assertions about the how and why of our hurt and offers us a path to liberation, to wholeness.

And, in service to this project of healing our broken hearts liberal Buddhism, and its Zen expression, while without a doubt harboring shadows, has enormous possibilities. Out of its broad inclination to identify with the ideals of science, we find a willingness to see the disciplines studied within scientific institutions. At first this was mostly in the realm of biofeedback studies. But, while these undoubtedly have value, they tend to be akin to studying a horse by examining its feces. Measurable relaxation or any other outcome is a by-product of Buddhism, not the thing itself.

But neuroscience has advanced considerably since the dawn of biofeedback, and we are beginning to be able to map many aspects of human consciousness, including perhaps where that larger perspective, the nondual insight, appears. But, still, while I am comforted to see the basic insights of a pre-scientific model of consciousness largely confirmed in an era of science, seeing the mechanisms is still like looking at a cookbook—we need to get into the kitchen and find out for ourselves.

The continued exploration of assumptions underlying liberal Buddhism and of the positive aspects of its secularization has resulted in a profound shift in emphasis supporting lay practice. In particular, the contours of Western Zen reveal a shift from Zen monastery to Zen center as the normative institution. These and other aspects of the liberal Buddhist perspective are compelling for many of us.

For instance, anyone visiting a range of Western Zen centers will find women at every level of leadership. And related to that, openly gay and lesbian people are almost uniformly accepted in these centers, often in leadership positions. This is all but unheard of in the East. And these are core perspectives of liberal Buddhism.

These new leaders and the perspectives they bring all help to create an even richer, more socially engaged vision of the Dharma than that which we inherited from our traditional teachers. Indeed, while it's calumny to claim Buddhism is "passive" and disengaged from the world, an inclination to withdrawal is indeed the shadow of Buddhism. Thus these social aspects of liberal Buddhism can particularly enrich our tradition.

Another potential problem that liberal Buddhism can possibly ameliorate is that Buddhist organizations in East Asia have usually worked with the approval and, in many instances, support of the state. In China monasteries were often supported by large land grants that included serfs, for all practical purposes slaves. In Japan, the ruling classes quickly saw how Zen, particularly Rinzai Zen, could be adapted to support the needs of the warrior class. This became a mutually reinforcing relationship; as anyone who cares to know knows, in the Second World War the Zen churches were second to none in their enthusiastic support of the imperialist assertions of emperor and state. The self-supporting independence of Buddhist sanghas in the West gives hope that such problems can be avoided. Although, no doubt, other problems will present instead.

Here in the West we must reflect on how this Zen Dharma might be engaged in the light of our own circumstances as inheritors of the Western traditions of Judaism, Christianity, and Humanism. Here the value of psychology becomes obvious, as does some historical sense, and a critical stance in regard to the events of our lives.

Here great insight of nonduality is actualized—as well as those powerful and transformative disciplines we've inherited on the Zen way.

Wrestling with Natural Law

WE HUMAN BEINGS are meant to categorize things; it's what our brains do. We make lists, we make judgments, we plan, we decide what is useful and what is not. So in our human societies we have some deep need to find who is "in" and who is "out"—and frequently that judgment is a moral one. This isn't simply an academic observation. Over the ages moral assertions believed to be derived from nature, but which are in fact simply about who is in and who is out, have led to numerous oppressions. Right off I can think of the subjugation of women and people of different colors and homosexual persons, not to mention left-handed people and folk with red hair.

And here's a hard fact to ignore: all these oppressions suggest that moral codes are too often little more than crowd control. How goes that old and sad joke? The golden rule means those with the gold rule. I find little doubt that much of morality is simply about power. Our moral rules that categorize people, that create castes, that define good and ill by color or gender, are rarely connected with the natural in any natural way, other than our natural inclination to categorize and to create in and out, pure and dirty, and to gather and to hold power.

All that acknowledged, still, the question hangs in the air, is there some moral code that can be called natural? Doesn't our common humanity take us to some deep-in-our-bones, written-on-our-hearts call to do this and to not do that?

I WAS WORKING IN A BOOKSTORE in San Diego and decided it was time to try a little college. In this context, I should perhaps mention that I am a high school drop out—so classes at a university were out of the question at this time. I went over to San Diego Evening College, which was only up the road a bit from the bookshop and had open registration. As it turned out, the only class available that was even vaguely interesting to me was something called "cultural anthropology." I'd really liked Edgar Rice Burroughs in my youth and had read several of his Tarzan books and so thought, what the heck, and signed up.

It was an eye-opener. I'd already picked up how people didn't all think the way I did. But I hadn't thought through what that might actually mean. Until, that is, I heard the term "cultural relativism." A friend illustrated this concept with a joke. It is in bad taste, but it makes the point. Perhaps before relating it I should add that I am largely of Irish descent.

An Englishman, an American, and an Irishman walked together into a bar and each ordered a beer. The bartender placed a frothy mug in front of each of them. Floating in each mug was a fly. The Englishman pushed the beer aside, declaring, "That's disgusting." The American pulled the fly out and started drinking his beer. The Irishman also pulled the fly out, set it on the counter, and shouted "You nasty little thing, spit out the rest of that beer!"

This little joke conveys some important points. Cultural stereotyping is rooted in how people from one culture see people from another. Beneath that, it points to how we see the world, and how that seeing is very much culturally bound. A culture is woven out of the stories we choose to tell about ourselves and about others. My sense is that the human mind itself is woven out of stories, my personal stories and the stories of my people. As I relentlessly witness the workings of my mind, I find I am very much a product of time and place. There is constraint, but also liberation.

Out of this I feel a deep need to notice how these stories are going to be different across the planet. Very much including, and this is so important, our stories of what is right and what is wrong. As such I think we need to cultivate a sense of cultural relativism. But cultural relativism isn't necessarily moral relativism. They're intertwined, no doubt. And I think the easy slide from one to the other by many of us, perhaps all of us at least on occasion, has been a mistake.

If there is any universal moral stance, ignoring it would have just as bad consequences as following false moral codes. Missing a deeper moral stance, if there is one, blinds us to who we are, you and I. And it blinds us to what goes on around the globe, and our place on this planet.

So, the question is hot. I know it burns deep in me. And the question is simple: is there really some universal morality beyond purity, beyond power? Is there something written on our hearts? In my spiritual quest, out of my years of introspection and observation, and profoundly cautioned about the consequences of misjudging, I've come to a conclusion.

I think the answer is yes.

As I search my heart and mind, as I look at people from around the world, I'm confident there is something deep within our human consciousness that births as judgments of "right" and "wrong" behavior, whether specifics stand up to close scrutiny or not. The first observable fact is that we all share a sense of right and wrong. I believe the source of our moral impulse is found within our biology—the fact that we are mammals, and specifically a herd variety of great ape. We are social animals, and that prejudices us toward relationships. We desperately need others.

But, I suspect very much, it also has much to do with the structure of our brains, with our innate quest for pattern, that amazing ability that has given us the planet on a silver platter. I believe our ability and our need to see pattern prejudices us toward order, and gives us all a sense of fairness, although the details of what that "fair" is are culturally specific.

Taken together, this becomes the mother source of our need for a moral life.

The devil, of course, lies in the details.

Perhaps the heart of the spiritual quest is the search for anything that can provide generally helpful rules as we try to live lives of worth and dignity.

Seven Suggestions

IN MY PERSONAL SEARCH for a universal moral code, I've long been fascinated by the Noahide code, a "universalist" list of precepts derived from the Hebrew scriptures, which is believed in some Jewish circles to be an expression of natural law. The Noahide code has seven precepts. One formulation goes:

1. Do not worship idols.
2. Do not blaspheme.
3. Do not commit murder.
4. Do not be sexually immoral.
5. Do not steal.
6. Pursue justice.
7. Do not be cruel to animals.

Framed more positively, they can be read:

1. Believe in God.
2. Respect and praise the divine.
3. Respect human life.
4. Respect your family.
5. Respect the rights of others.
6. Work for justice.
7. Respect animals.

The Buddha made a similar list: the Five Precepts he prescribed for his lay followers. He said these were part of the prescription for curing the ills of our human condition, curing the hurt of the human heart. The five precepts are:

1. Do not kill.
2. Do not lie.
3. Do not steal.
4. Do not misuse sex.
5. Do not become intoxicated.

As with the Noahide code, these precepts can also be formulated positively:

1. Foster life.
2. Speak truthfully.
3. Respect boundaries.
4. Respect your body and others' bodies.
5. Remain clear and open.

I find it intriguing where the Noahide and Buddhist precepts overlap and where they do not. Both have prohibitions about killing, for instance. Although for one it appears to be more narrowly a prohibition of unlawful killing of human beings specifically and for the other it is a rather more absolute instruction of no killing at all. There are also shared precepts about stealing and about sex, although again what exactly these mean is often expressed differently. The Noahide code upholds relationship with a creator, devoting two precepts to this, and calls for justice among human beings and kindness to animals. The Buddhist code is unconcerned with questions of deity, and instead upholds clarity of mind.

Since the details of any hopeful universal moral code are so obviously slippery, I've come to feel therefore they must be approached with caution. Nevertheless, as I've continued to ruminate on the subject, seven suggestions have come bubbling up as possible universal precepts reflecting the deep needs arising within our human condition—seven natural rules for human behavior. They are principally derived from the Buddha's five lay precepts, enriched by reflecting on the Noahide code. Each feels worthy of deeper reflection.

1. LOVE YOUR MOTHER. Here, as a Zen person, I try to articulate the sense of deep harmony that I find in those ancient calls to know and love God. I don't have a deep visceral sense of a personal deity—in fact anything that is obviously a projection of humanity into the sky I find pretty off-putting—but I do have a compelling sense of a larger sacredness of which I am simply, but wildly, and totally a part.

   This is something that I feel can easily be called God. It manifests as an abiding sense of sacred obligation to others and to the world. For various reasons, I find that simply shifting the gender of "God" can help people in our time and place shake loose from the old-man-in-the-sky idea of god, to broaden and enliven the engagement. Here we might encounter Gaia, our mother earth, the substance of our substance. And so the precept is to love our mother.

2. REVERENCE LIFE. Here we need to see into the mystery of life and death, of the great conundrum that eating requires killing, that we cannot take a walk without killing thousands of life forms. And, always, how within

the embrace of our mother we are all one family, and how actually the truth is even more radical—we are one. We need to see the connections and seek to walk with care and gratitude.

3. SPEAK TRUTHFULLY. Words have enormous power; words create and destroy. We need to be careful with our words. We need to speak what is helpful, generous, and kind. For the most part we need to let our yes be yes and our no, no.

4. RESPECT THINGS. There is a profound conundrum to life. While in a very true sense we are completely interdependent and one can accurately say we are one, at the same time we are different: you are you and I am I. Here our Western logic sometimes fails us; just like energy is now a wave and now a particle, we are now one and now separate. This precept is a call to respect. We need to respect boundaries, even if they are in some ultimate sense provisional. And we need to acknowledge the various claims people have within these boundaries.

5. RESPECT OUR BODIES. We need to know and respect and love ourselves; in particular we need to know and respect and love ourselves as sexual beings. And we need to extend that knowledge and respect and love to others' bodies, as well.

6. SEEK JUSTICE. In our communal lives we need to seek equity and harmony. We need to respect the individual and to know we have common needs. No one is an island.

7. SEEK CLARITY. In order to manifest this harmonious life, we need to remain clear. We need to be watchful of those things that cloud our perceptions, that lead to false conclusions and unhealthy actions. We need to foster those things that extend our clarity and allow our actions to be more generous and harmonious with the way things are.

These precepts or suggestions or pointers will be further explored in the ensuing chapters. Many of those chapters will begin with a quotation from the Boundless Way Zen precepts ceremony, drawing on the words of the ancient masters Bodhidharma and Dogen, and on other sources too. For each precept, each guideline, I'll try to hold up one or more of the three ways of engagement we find in Zen Buddhism: a literal understanding, a more dynamic and compassionate understanding, or that absolute, empty, or boundless understanding—that place where the terms and distinctions fade away like an old painting under a bright sun. Each has its place in our understanding of our codes, now a rule, now a frame, now simply an expression of the vast *is*, the great not knowing.

Do Not Cut Yourself Off from This World

■ LOVE YOUR MOTHER ■

If you meet the Buddha
you meet the Goddess.
If you meet the Goddess
you meet the Buddha.

■ RICK FIELDS ■
FROM "THE VERY SHORT SUTRA ON THE
MEETING OF THE BUDDHA AND THE GODDESS"

I WAS RAISED a fundamentalist Baptist. The god of my child-hood was a stern patriarch, not very likable, quite distant, and mainly someone to fear. At first the only alternative I was aware of was the bare-bones atheism embodied by my father, which for a while I embraced. But neither position—fear or denial—seemed particularly fulfilling, either emo-tionally or intellectually. That word *god* seemed to stand for so many things; just because some meanings didn't work, it still didn't feel like the word should or could be set aside without significant loss. There was just too much about it that needed, that needs, investigation. And so I continued on, following a pretty fervent but engaged agnosticism, occa-sionally tipping toward belief, more usually not.

I do believe the questions of God are very big, very important. And right from the start one can see the difficulties. For instance I've been teased of late by a few friends about the fact that when I refer to the divine in my capacity as a Unitarian Universalist minister it seems obvious I'm rather more inclined to the metaphor "mother" than "father." Those who know my family history think that settles the why of it, and I'm sure there is some truth to their theory. But, as with most of life, I suggest this is a rather more complicated affair, not so easily reducible to a single cause.

In my late teens, I stumbled upon the story of Ramakrishna, a nineteenth century Hindu saint. He was a Bengali and a priest of the goddess Kali, whose name means "the black one." I very much identified with his fervent desire to know his goddess. He pursued her with all his energy. And in this short version of the telling, eventually he was gifted with a vision. In his vision the goddess emerged from a river, swollen with pregnancy, gave birth to a child, and then ate it. I read this and it took my breath away. I was repulsed and at the very same time felt somewhere deep inside me that this was a spiritual pointing to something more profound than I had ever before dreamt.

Ramakrishna himself, when commenting on this vision, taught, "My Mother is the principle of consciousness. She is indivisible Reality, Awareness, and Bliss. The night sky between the stars is perfectly black. The waters of the ocean depths are the same; the infinite is always mysteriously dark. This inebriating darkness is my beloved Kali."

This was my initial encounter with an idea of the divine that pushed the conventional spiritual boundaries of a god that was separate from the world. And at that boundary I found a gate. I looked through it and I saw something much bigger, not entirely pleasant—not at all—but enormously compelling. For me, deeply compelling. And I rushed on through that gate. I've never regretted it.

Later I would stumble upon the writings of the seventeenth-century Jewish philosopher Baruch Spinoza. And I began to find words for what I was experiencing. In my heart Spinoza remains one of the greatest of Western teachers. He noticed the unity of all things, starting with a reconciliation of mind and matter. He saw that nature and God are two different names for the same thing. And he raised troubling questions, at least for me, about free will and determinism. No doubt he challenged our conventional Western ideas of what is. And pushed me ever further on my quest.

I'm collapsing the chronology a bit, but all of this led me into a Buddhist monastery, and years of watching my mind and its intimate workings. It led to that taste of a cabbage leaf. It lead to many more small and large openings. It led to the way. Along this way probably the most important technique I found for this investigation was koan study. Earlier, I unpacked a bit what a koan might be for us on our spiritual quest. I suggest we can best use the word *god* as a koan.

The word *god* holds everything we intuit about the world and what might be beyond. I've come to think of that word *god* as a hole in the language into which we throw all our fears and hopes. A friend heard me say that and asked if I meant a whole in the language. Hole. Whole. The answer is yes. In the discipline that is koan work one usually encounters the matter in at least three ways, as Robert Aitken has framed it: the literal, the essential, and the compassionate.

First, literal. This is the God revealed. Each religion presents it a bit differently. An investigation of the Christian scriptures shows what looks like an evolutionary arc of the understanding of the divine revealed in different strata of the texts. It can be like an archeological dig: at the oldest revealing a storm god, later the god of a people, and still later a universal God, a loving parent to the whole of creation. If we take this as a koan we need to encounter all the contradictions. And there is always that terrible question: How can a loving God be involved in the evil we see around us?

I believe in some ways Spinoza is also an example of this literal engagement. When Albert Einstein was asked whether he believed in God, he replied, "I believe in Spinoza's God who reveals himself in the orderly harmony of what exists, not in a God who concerns himself with the fates and actions of human beings." Of course the world isn't completely orderly, and what happens among human beings is for us as human beings the ultimate matter.

The literal has enormous value. It is the realm where we divide the universe, weigh, consider, and make choices. And in considering ultimacy there certainly are questions, there certainly are challenges. What about the reality of evil? Who can read a newspaper and not think about evil? And what about the fact the world isn't completely orderly? The deeper we look, the weirder it gets, weirder and weirder right down to the bottom. Rich subjects, worth considering, worth following right down to the bottom.

But, if we leave the idea of God to this realm alone, I believe we miss something very important. For me Spinoza is best when he is pointing toward something beyond the analysis. And in fact he did call each of us to our own intimate, what he called "intuitive," insight. This spirit is found in just about every traditional religion, as well. It is the call of the mystics, another problematic word that contains within a mess of uses the meaning of a sorority, a fraternity of practitioners of depth.

Of course this is the call for all of us, to find ways to look fiercely into our own hearts and minds, to see through to the heart of the matter. That is, I believe, a deep responsibility we are all charged with at our birth. This takes me to that second thing, after literal, to what might be the "essential" of God. I throw the quotes around essential because it is another problematic word. Here I don't mean some supra essence, but am in fact trying to point to another place entirely.

And this brings us back to Kali, back to black. I speak frequently of embracing humility in spiritual practice, of only not knowing. There is a powerful method in this. But it isn't just a method; it is also a destination. In Western theological terms, it is *kenosis*, emptiness, nothingness, the divine darkness that is, for many, the womb of the universe.

We find it when we really, really let go of our knowing, of our analysis, of our grasping after this and fearing that. Words fail here, because words are part of the literal. Still, people who have walked the way have found words that point. "Black" is one. "Cloud of unknowing" is another. "Beginner's mind," another. "Only don't know" can also be heard as pointing to this place. And many, many have found it, that place where "it" and all other designations melt away like ice on a summer sidewalk.

However, we don't appear to be meant to live there in that place beyond words. Those who have walked this way mostly have fleeting insights into this realm, place, stance. A few live more commonly there, but they, I notice often, don't function all that well here in the world of choices. This place, I think, is meant to be visited, but not to be lived in.

Visiting the essential realm then takes us to the realm of the compassionate, where the literal and the essential reconcile. And that is usually the third point in any koan, and it certainly seems so very true for our encounter with the koan God.

In Zen there is a map of the spiritual way called the "Ten Ox-Herding Pictures." There are several versions. The one I find most helpful shows a boy chasing after an ox, catching it, taming it, and riding it home. The first steps are all about our literal encounter: the boy capturing and riding the ox. Near the end, both boy and ox disappear, first into an empty circle and then to a simple nature scene without a boy or an ox. These pictures are about the essential. The last encounter, comprised of only one picture, shows a fat man walking into a village carrying a bag. There are various traditional captions; my favorite is "returning to the world with bliss-bestowing hands." That is the third encounter, the compassionate. And the unraveling of what that "returning to the world with bliss-bestowing hands" means can take up an entire lifetime.

And, I suggest, it should.

Here we discover ourselves walking the divine way. Here we find our actions informed by choices that themselves are grounded in a realization of our true commonality, our true reconciliation, yours and mine, in something vastly larger than our grandest dreams.

Here we find that God is our father, is our mother, is our brother, sister, son, and daughter—and our friends and enemies too. Here we find how truly we really are all one family, how we really are all one, and what is done to the least is done to all.

That's the world we're called to.

Do Not Kill

> Recognizing that I am not separate from all that is, I
> take up the way of Not Killing. Self-nature is subtle
> and mysterious. In the realm of everlasting Dharma,
> not giving rise to the idea of killing is called the Pre-
> cept of Not Killing. The Buddha's seed grows in accor-
> dance with not taking life. Transmit the life of
> Buddha's wisdom and do not kill.
>
> ■ BOUNDLESS WAY ZEN PRECEPTS CEREMONY ■

1.

MY UNDERSTANDING is that the Jewish and Christian commandment to not kill is a very nuanced thing. Depending
on which list you prefer, it is the fifth or sixth commandment of the ten best known ones, which are in turn generally considered the most important of some six hundred
twenty-three commandments found in the Hebrew Scriptures. The most common interpretation of this particular
commandment is that we are not to murder, i.e., not to commit an unlawful killing of another person. Some do take it
to be a more comprehensive call; a few even see a call to
pacifism within it. But this larger view appears to be a
minority report.

This is not so for the Buddhist precept about killing, which is unambiguous, and therefore, of course, ultimately impossible. In Buddhism everything has a place, and all living things are cherished; the precept is an unmodified, not nuanced statement: do not kill—anything, ever. Even in pre-scientific ages it was pretty obvious that walking and breathing involve at least the possibility of killing. Few missed this. And as time advanced and we began to understand the wealth of life that disappears with each step, with each breath, its impossibility loomed ever larger. But even from the beginning, as one faces the necessities of eating, well, the problems in this precept just pile one upon another.

So, a literal understanding is going to be of limited use. As I write these words the church community to which I belong has experienced a suicide. In addition to the circumstances that led someone to climb over a barrier and jump off a parking structure, the hurt and guilt and confusion of those left behind has been a terrible thing. And I assure you I'm not separate from those feelings. There are always consequences to our actions, and killing self or other seems to leave in its wake more powerful disconnections than most things we do.

So, what about suicide? What about war? What about euthanasia? What about capital punishment? What about abortion? What about eating anything, but particularly eating meat?

Worthy questions all: each investigates life and death, and each speaks also of unique situations, and each raises questions that cannot with any integrity be conflated into the others. And none, that I can see, lends itself to a simple "you can't do this under any circumstances" or "don't worry about it." There is something of a tragic cast to our lives.

And I feel these questions of navigating the deep waters of life and death and our hand in life and death are where we see that tragedy most obviously.

And so I think the call in this precept is to engage. To not look away, diminish, or minimize. The heart of the matter, of our own lives, and the lives of those around us, those we care for, and those we hate, or who hate us, is where we find life and death meeting. This is the meeting. Just life. Just death. Just life-and-death—one thing. Just this moment, filled with loss and gain, despair and hope. And prepared or not, we're called in each moment to make decisions that are in fact about life and death. Every moment is that important.

And as I sit with this precept, I don't actually find that it is about the world being red in tooth and claw. Rather, it is about how we are all joined together in the great rhythm of life and death, the great circle itself. But we are also gifted with awareness of what is happening—or at least a large portion of what is happening—and hence are culpable. We are responsible in a way no other creature I'm aware of is. We have eaten of the fruit of the knowledge of good and evil, and we have become as gods. And that godlike quality is responsibility.

I find this precept a call to meet the world and our actions in it with relentless honesty—and a certain gentleness.

//.

Jesus, at least in the King James version of his words, is said to have spoken a famous phrase about "war and rumors of war." Some take it as prophecy, about how things will be. But, of course, it's actually about how things are. There have been no times in our human history without the organized killing of human beings happening somewhere. In the years since 9/11 we Americans are particularly, painfully, and intimately aware of this terrible reality.

I find it impossible to avoid reflecting on this endless warring, our human propensity for violence, and what it might mean. A good place to start might be to ask how we come to find ourselves in this pickle. I look into my own heart and see some of that source.

Some years past when Jan and I lived in Newton, Massachusetts, I was shopping at the Star Market. In addition to picking up some necessities and the makings for that evening's dinner, I was purchasing some beer. While I don't drink, Jan does imbibe upon occasion, mostly wine, but when the weather is right she likes a beer. This was beer season and I take pleasure in shopping around to find designer beers for her to sample. On this trip I saw I could select from among the micro- and slightly-less-than-macro-brews while still getting a single six-pack price. A mix-and-match deal.

I got in line at the cash register. It was a fair wait. Then, finally at the register, apparently the very young person checking the groceries hadn't encountered this six-pack mix-and-match possibility. She held up one of the six bottles I'd gathered and asked, "How much?" I replied, "I don't exactly remember, but a sign said the assortment comes at a single six-pack price."

This led to calling over a manager, a brief discussion, and then a trip for another pimply-faced youth to the beer department. Now the line behind me, as you might have gathered, was backing up, and people were beginning to twitch. So, I was feeling the pressure. Everything else was rung up, and we waited on that price for what seemed to be an eternity, except, actually, a bit longer.

At last the guy standing directly behind me, a fellow in a

blue pinstripe suit with his tie loosened, spoke up. "Hey, this seems like a fifty-cent deal. I'll pay the damn fifty cents! Let's get going."

I flushed with embarrassment. I turned to him and said, indignantly, "We're just trying to find the price." He snorted derisively and looked at his wristwatch. Something big and gold, I decided it probably was a Rolex. I turned my back again to avoid his and everyone else's gaze, but my mind stayed focused on the guy with the Rolex. Standing there, I found myself running through all sorts of scenarios, none of which seemed appropriate to either a minister or a Zen practitioner. But here I admit it to you—violence was definitely part of my thought process.

Finally, excruciatingly, the wait came to an end. I did, indeed, find myself paying an extra fifty cents. I left the store red as the proverbial beet, from my hairline right down to my collar, and my mind filled with murderous thoughts.

So, what's the deal? How is it that a well-socialized, more or less good citizen, minister, and Zen practitioner, finds quite violent thoughts bubbling in his skull, at least one of which featured a corpse with a Rolex lying in a grocery store checkout line? What's the story there? Let me tell you, I've ruminated on this scene for years. And I continue to find it troubling.

Thinking about it deeply doesn't lead to the happiest conclusions. There's a recent play called *Hominid* produced at Emory University in Atlanta. It touches on the problem as well. I heard a story about it on NPR. Later I went to the web and looked it up. Emory provided a plot outline.

A conniving kingmaker and his young protégé conspire to overthrow a popular king. Their plot fails, so they murder him instead. The kingmaker then installs his protégé as ruler. The young king does not properly reward his mentor, however, so the kingmaker selects a new protégé. Together, they torment the young king to the point of madness. He throws himself into the palace moat and drowns.

The reason you can't quite put your finger upon which of Shakespeare's works inspired this play is because it's actually based upon real events that took place at a nature preserve in the 1970s. The characters, I should mention, are all chimpanzees. If this doesn't bother you, you're not paying attention. We share nearly all our DNA with chimps. That we humans and chimps both play out Shakespearean tragedies is important information, very important information.

There is a dilemma at the heart of our human condition. For instance, from looking at how we organize ourselves, its obvious we're herd animals; we have a deep biological need to cooperate. And yet we cheat. All the time. Also, as possibly the only animal to anticipate our own deaths, we have a deep knowing that death causes cascades of hurt for many, and is in some real, visceral, and terrible way wrong. And yet we kill. Both by our actions and by how we refrain from action. Our contradictory inclinations are inherent in us, part of the deal of being alive, of being human, of being an ape, of being a mammal.

Of course, we're the reflective animal. We watch ourselves and we think about it. Human beings have wrestled with what all this means for the entirety of our existence; probably, I would say almost certainly, from the moment we first formed a sentence. For the most part we've done this wrestling within the frame of our religious traditions. And our visions are many. The ancient Norse, for instance, saw any harmonies as fragile and predicted an inevitable decline into chaos. Most religions, however, seek reconciliation between the poles of our lives. This reconciled heart is found in different ways, some I've found more useful, others less so.

One feature of our way is to look wide for guidance. Here I find myself thinking of the great Hindu classic the Bhagavad Gita. I suspect most know the broad outline of the story. There's a terrible fratricidal civil war. As the culminating battle prepares, the prince Arjuna despairs, and orders his charioteer to drive him to the open space between the gathering armies. Quickly it becomes apparent that the charioteer is in fact Krishna, God. With that revelation they speak of fundamental matters.

For me the least satisfactory part of the story is when Krishna tells Arjuna his fate is to fight and to win. Arjuna is told the heroes of the other side were already dead even before the first sword is raised. It is all God's will. I have to admit, as a justification for terrible things, "God's will" has never impressed me. It's a bit too much like the bare story of Job where it seems, in the face of all the terrible things that happen, he's told by God to shut up and submit. It's all God's will.

But like the story of Job, where a deeper answer can in fact be seen as something vastly more than a demand to bow down in the dust, the story of Arjuna is often seen as a call to something rather deeper than obey and kill. In both cases there is a call to presence, to not turning away, and a promise of a larger vision that can and will come out of that full presence to the moment, to this moment in which we actually live. It is a call to wisdom.

This calls us to a vision where nothing is excluded, and opens us to genuine wisdom. It is an ecstatic vision, although a terrible one, in the fullness of that word. Here's my suggestion. For just a moment, set aside the idea that our suffering is meant to educate us. Set aside the idea that death is a door to some other place. Set aside the words, all the words that tumble from us, and with them the meanings, small and large, which the words give to things. Just be present. Don't forget the hurt. Don't forget the joy. Don't forget the killing. Don't forget each birth. Be present and know this moment, full, just this moment. Just for a moment.

I suggest that by being fully here, not turning away, within the great roil of reality, something appears at the center of things, birthing within our hearts as a deep knowing—or perhaps it is better to call it a profound not-knowing. We become open. Now, flawed or not, the words will come again. This is our human condition, to think, to wrestle with it, to find meaning of one sort or another. The words come.

> Arjuna saw the whole universe
> enfolded, with its countless billions
> of life-forms, gathered together
> in the body of the God of gods.

Here are words informed by that deathless place, that moment of not knowing, open to all. We are one within the web. We are unique and different, and we are one within the web.

With this deep knowledge of our connectedness, of our intimate relationships, with the man with the Rolex watch, with Osama bin Laden, with the chimps, with the turkey that was featured at many people's most recent Thanksgiving dinner, with every blessed thing on this planet, with the killers and the killed—we notice and a door opens. We are not excused from action; in a world that is completely interdependent, to where can we absent ourselves? We must make decisions. We must act. This is part of the deal. But our ancient inclination to violence will also be challenged, be informed by our deep knowing we are all related.

Know the connections and we open up, becoming as wide as the universe. With that our individual hearts turn, and our actions become something more gentle, more kind, more just. If, as the oracle tells us, we truly know ourselves, then we will walk this world with grace, chimps that have found wisdom.

Do Not Lie

■ SPEAK TRUTHFULLY ■

Listening and speaking from the heart, I vow to take up
the Way of Not Speaking Falsely. Self-nature is subtle
and mysterious. In the realm of the inexplicable Dharma,
not preaching a single word is called the Precept of Not
Speaking Falsely. The Dharma Wheel turns and turns.
There is neither surplus nor lack. The whole universe is
moistened with nectar, and the truth is ready to harvest.

■ BOUNDLESS WAY ZEN PRECEPTS CEREMONY ■

1.

PONTIUS PILATE famously washed his hands of the matter
of the crucifixion of Jesus with the rhetorical question,
"What is truth?" My rummaging around for the original
uses of the word *truth* has found a constellation of words
that call for faithfulness, some of which, searching for a pre–
Indo-European root, look to the word *tree*, as in the
metaphor, "steadfast as an oak."

I write these words in an ironic age, where notions of truth
are at best slippery things. Is there anything as steadfast as
an oak in our lives? Is there anything to anchor us? Where
do we find truth and falsehood? What can it look like?

James Boswell, in his *Life of Johnson*, recalls:

> After we came out of the church, we stood talk-
> ing for some time together of Bishop Berkeley's
> ingenious sophistry to prove the non-existence of
> matter, and that everything in the universe is mere-
> ly ideal. I observed that though we are satisfied
> his doctrine is not true, it is impossible to refute
> it. I never shall forget the alacrity with which
> Johnson answered, striking his foot with mighty
> force against a large stone, till he rebounded from
> it, "I refute it *thus*."

Now there's a question of truth being presented in an
almost Zen-like way. Although the Anglican theologian and
physicist John Polkinghorne throws some cold water on that
response that I think we should attend to. "Dr. Johnson," he
tells us, "kicking the stone to refute Bishop Berkeley will
not do. That stone is almost all empty space and what is not
is a weaving of wave-mechanical patterns." And while I just
love Johnson's this-worldly response, I believe Dr. Polkinghorne is closer to the truth. And, noticing how I respond to
this assessment, I see how I believe in truth. Or, at least,
something moving in that direction…

I do not engage the world with ironic distance. I'm deeply
moved by the solidity of that kick, by the reality of my touching my wife, by the substance of my drinking a cup of cof-
fee with friends. And, at the very same time, I'm profoundly
informed by a body knowing that everything is passing,
nothing has an essential substance. And I'm sure that knowing both truths as the creative tension of life is the way of

authentic relationship with each other, with ourselves, with the world, with all of it.

As I consider my life and how to live it, I find that a certain fidelity in relationships is essential. I need to speak the truth as best I understand it—not just as a sign of my commitment to the relationship, but as an essential element of the relationship in itself. And I must at the same time hold my view of the truth lightly; it is critical to remember that what I know to be true is always, always contingent.

Someone once asked an old friend of mine, a Dharma bum who often prefers the moniker Weasel Tracks, "Do you believe in God?" Uncle Weasel replied, "No." The person pursued the matter, and asked, "So, you're an atheist?" To which the ever-slippery Zen guy said, "No." Frustrated, the questioner demanded to know, "What do you believe?" To which my friend simply replied, "As little as possible."

We should be careful of what we believe, and hold what we come to feel we must believe as lightly as possible.

Here is the modesty of truth as a spiritual way:

It isn't about rules. It isn't about clinging to whatever just because. It is about our hearts being open, and our faithful following of the great way, all the way down.

//.

In my distress I called to the Lord, and he answered me.
Deliver me, O Lord, from lying lips,
from a deceitful tongue.

■ PSALM 120 ■

It is hard to believe a man is telling the truth when you
know that you would lie if you were in his place.

■ H.L. MENCKEN ■

My father had a rough life. It included little formal education, maybe up to the third grade. Still he clearly was very intelligent, read a lot, and had an aptitude for both math and language. I know that when he was in jail during my early teen years he tutored his fellow inmates in both basic English and arithmetic skills. I remember that when I learned what he was doing I thought when he got out of jail he would become a schoolteacher, and our lives would change. There were many things I didn't understand. Still true...

Anyway, he loved science fiction. And through him, so did I. In fact I consider science fiction my first window on a larger world than the very constricted one in which we actually lived. At some point he started writing his own stories. He would make carbon copies and pass them around to friends, and to me. I was thrilled and would encourage him to send them off to the magazines we read, like *Amazing Stories* and *Fantasy and Science Fiction*. Then one day after reading a story he'd written, I was rummaging through the boxes of old magazines he kept and found one that contained the story I had just read. Not, of course, written by him.

For years I've brooded over the wounds in his heart that led to those fake stories. Similarly I serve a church where my predecessor was discovered to be a plagiarist, stealing not only other people's sermons but also critical autobiographical details that he presented as his own life. Events that he described as informing who he was were fabrications. I find it hard to see what circumstances could transpire where he should ever be allowed to serve as a parish minister again, and I am also aware that he is someone who, within all his hurts, wanted desperately to serve. While I see the damage, and know the need for truthfulness, I feel sympathy for the wounds that led to these transgressions.

That moment of sympathy allows me to see all sorts of reasons I might lie. For one, I know I'm capable of lying in a moment of embarrassment, such as when confronted with something I didn't actually get around to doing, even though I said I would and thought I would, and will in a minute or two. Other lies are any number of small social encounters that really seem necessary for human relationships: "Yes, you look great," for instance. And, at the other end, I've seen people use truth as a club to simply beat others down, to no obvious good and to much obvious ill. I fear I've done that, as well. So lies sometimes even seem appropriate. And truth sometimes seems wrong.

I think about that a lot. I am not calling for Pilate's washing his hands while asking, "What is truth?" Rather, I suggest we approach this matter in another way. I suggest that somewhere in our feeling lives, somewhere below the reason, there is a call to truth. But it is contained within such a mess, that mess of flesh and blood, mind and heart, histories and circumstances—that mess of living contradiction, all haunted by our mortality.

Alfred North Whitehead had a similar thought when he observed that all truths are half-truths. We do see through that glass darkly. Certainly as I consider the nature of truth, I see all the bad news of it, or at least the astonishing complexity of it. I see the practical effect of truth telling, even without appeal to special revelation. And at the same time it is inescapably relative and situational. But I also think there is something deeper here, something very important— a compass, a sense that informs the situation.

I'm deeply informed by the dynamic I've observed in life of our human ability to see how the world is made of distinct things, the "you" as distinct from "me," and yet at the very same time we have this astonishing intuition that transcends cultures and religions, that is glimpsed in moments, but that completely transforms lives—an intuition that we are also in some profound sense truly one. It is my belief that the sense of oneness is the secret. The Japanese philosopher Kitaro Nishida frames how this works in his observation that our "knowledge of things in the world begins with the differentiation of unitary consciousness into knower and known and ends with self and things becoming one again." He goes from there to suggest how our sense of unity informs our sense of value, and that sense gives us sympathy for the other, which itself gives rise to our desire to act in this world of differentiation toward a larger good. This seems roughly right to me. If you will, this is the truth.

Lies then are how we deceive ourselves about our essential unity. For a short moment or a whole lifetime, we deny ourselves our connection with others, and from that fundamental lie, all the little ones flow. Some of those lies are actually not all that little, as we know. With each lie, small or large, comes hurt. Perhaps there's a short-term gain, that's almost always the motive, but it involves diminishment of ourselves as well reinforcing a false view of the world around us.

So, there we are, here we are. As seems to be the case in most of these principles of life—like not killing and not stealing and not lying—there are at least three ways we need to engage the matter. First, there are the plain rules of it; don't lie. Second, there is also a place where all ideas collapse and truth and lies fall apart, and all that is left is the vastness itself. And third, where these things return in a dance, a dynamic, in our actual lived lives, we find that deeper reality to which the rule "don't lie" points, when we see we are one even as we are multiple, and when I lie to you I am lying to myself.

At one moment one aspect is paramount, at another, another. But like life itself, in the great play of things, on this stage we share together where each takes a part, there is a wholeness that is bigger, that allows us to see what is happening, and that draws us to rewrite the script.

Because of this dynamic, there is hope. We can let go of the lies in our hearts, particularly that worst of all lies, that we are separate. And informed by a spirit of truthfulness, we can find each moment created anew, and possibility waiting, the world pregnant with hope.

That I think is the truthfulness we seek, and which awaits our turned hearts.

Do Not Steal

> Being satisfied with what I have, I vow to take up the Way of Not Stealing. Self-nature is subtle and mysterious. In the realm of the unattainable Dharma, not having thoughts of gaining is called the Precept of Not Stealing. The self and the things of the world are just as they are. The gate of emancipation is open.
>
> ■ BOUNDLESS WAY ZEN PRECEPTS CEREMONY ■

1.

PROBABLY my all-time favorite reflection on the bodhisattva precepts is Robert Aitken's little volume *Mind of Clover: Essays in Zen Buddhist Ethics*. Published in 1984, it was the first full book in the English language to deal with ethical issues from a Zen perspective.

In that volume the old roshi listed various types of theft, such as the theft of time, for instance when we find ourselves on the meditation cushion and instead of attending to the matter at hand, just being present, we plan or scheme or fantasize. This is the theft of leaping ahead or behind this present moment to something else, and thus wasting the moment that was.

He went on to describe the exploitation of others as theft.

An old socialist, Aitken Roshi observed, "Stealing is a pervasive element of our lives, and is the nature of our economic system." While I agree with the first part of that sentence, I think one can argue about the second half. Not that there aren't problems with capitalism. But I suggest greed is the problematic aspect of American-style capitalism, not theft.

For me the take-away lesson is that we need to be careful about how we define things. The old line from anarchist Pierre-Joseph Proudhon that property is theft isn't so obvious to me. As part of the project of awakening, which is at the heart of the precepts, being careful about what is yours and mine and figuring out what exactly is yours and mine is not, I think, the heart of the matter.

Rather, the call is to two things. First, it is a call to a certain contentment with who we are, as we are. And yes, this call to deeply accept reality can become a call to not rock economic or political boats; religions can do that. They are frequently the bastions of the status quo, too often dressing up old evils in liturgical garb. But this is an abuse of the real point, which is how this world here and now is home. And our at-home-ness is found only here. Right here.

Second, we're called to an acknowledgment that, in this home, even as we are one we are also many. And the "many" is not a generic "many." It is the pile of books on either side of me. The phone. The small picture of Mary Magdalene as a sage holding an egg that hangs above the computer as I type these words. And the computer itself. And each individual key on the keyboard. As well as the fingers dashing along.

Not stealing is respecting the thingness of the world; each thing, as it is.

Just this.

11.

Again returning to my fundamentalist Baptist upbringing: among the more interesting things about the Baptists—and the source of their denominational name—is the concept of adult baptism, as opposed to baptism shortly after birth. They felt a person had to have his or her own intimate experience of salvation before undergoing the ritual, which was full body immersion—which, for us, involved a large bathtub built into the platform where the preacher preached, and which when not in use was discretely hidden by a curtain.

The catch to this is that "adult," for purposes of baptism, was about eleven or twelve in our community. Not, frankly, what I consider to be an age of discernment. In fact I recall being strongly encouraged, if not outright coerced, by various adults around me to "be saved," as we called the experience they wanted me to have. As the eldest child, I knew my responsibility. However, when I finally declared myself to be ready, to the relief of many, and the date was set for the ceremony, my greatest anxiety had to do with rocket ships.

You see, my friends and I had discovered you could cut shingles into a sort of aerodynamic wing, and then nail the ends of an inner tube to two large planks to create a giant slingshot, and really launch those shingle rockets into the air and nearly out of sight. The catch was the way we obtained those shingles: we stole them from local construction sites. And according to the doctrines of our branch of the church, one could not, physically and literally could not, sin once baptized. For those who care about such things, this doctrine is called perfectionism and it must have come to us through the Methodists.

So this was a major theological crisis, perhaps my first, although not, I admit, my last. My friends and I dealt with this spiritual conundrum by stealing as many shingles as we could hide right up to the day of the baptism, safe in the knowledge that even if we couldn't sin after baptism, we'd have a lifetime supply of shingles waiting. I thought I was home free. What followed was a year or two with only minor moral infractions—a couple of small lies, being mean to my brother, that sort of thing—none of which seemed particularly important to me. And then puberty happened, and sexuality entered my life. That's when I was introduced to the finer points of guilt and shame. Not to mention a serious concern about the fires of hell.

Theft, taking what is not yours, and its consequences have varied over the years and in different cultures. We've all heard old stories about peasants being executed for stealing bread, and as recently as 1801 a thirteen-year-old was executed in England for stealing a spoon. If you dig into the back pages of newspapers you can find extreme examples somewhere in the world even today. So one might expect various criticisms of property and defenses of theft. And there certainly have been: Proudhon, for instance, with his "property is theft."

A more common confusion for people is who is the thief. As Woody Guthrie sang, "Some will rob you with a six-gun. Some with a fountain pen." My grandmother, blessings upon her name, a Missouri native, believed the James boys (Jesse et al.) were driven to crime by the banks. There's a whole current of legend and fact about people who steal from the rich in order to save the poor. And, of course, there are mixed feelings about it. I have a friend, a pure libertarian, who told me if someone was starving and the choice was to steal from someone else in order to feed him—such as, for instance, taxing the other person to provide food for the starving one—or to let him starve, then morally, one should let the person starve. Lord save us from the pure.

Clearly, there is a range of opinion about what actually is theft and its import in the greater scheme of things. Well, somewhere within that mix—where on the one hand ownership of things is so absolute that someone who steals should be killed, and where on the other property is simply a means of controlling people—I believe we can find something important.

I suspect the first perspective, and its variations, has to do with our sense of autonomy, of self. Now it is my considered opinion (though of course not mine alone) that self, yours and mine, is in fact a construction; it has no existence outside of context. We are woven out of many things. These include genes and experiences. And out of that for mysterious reasons a person happens, out of that mix of conditions a sense of identity arises. Me, you, each of us is a moment where the universe sees itself, or at least a part of itself. And within this sense of awareness of that self, we also tend to see our boundaries at our skin. But in fact, in our actual experience, that's not completely so. Our various senses extend who we are, our actual boundaries, if you think about it, well beyond our skin. While the boundaries are fuzzy, the sense of self is not, at least if we're lucky and healthy. And our sense of possession, of ownership of things, is simply part of our sense of self, extended beyond our skin. Our ideas of property, of things we own, have a lot to do with that extension of who we see we are.

Similarly, because we are woven out of many things, out of each other and out of the world itself, when we look even more closely it is often not at all clear where any lines are, where anything is that is not connected, deeply and truly.

This is because, actually, there are no lines. The whole blessed cosmos is connected. We are all one family. And actually that extends beyond the biological—we are cousins to lizards and microbes, to stars and to the dirt.

And at some level we all know this. At various moments in our lives we may well have flashes of intimation, small and sometimes grand encounters with how everything is connected. But, for the most part the sense of oneness is weaker than our sense of separation, of self. Without serious attention, often requiring serious spiritual disciplines, we tend to forget, or to simply be unaware of this part of us. Still, even when this reality is far from our consciousness, it informs us at the body-knowing level. It is the great source of our need for harmony and the idea of fairness that seems to be held common by human beings.

The separation part, as I said, comes easier. In the normal course of things we are pretty aware of being distinct, of having boundaries. And we are pretty fragile creatures— throughout our lives we are in constant danger of breaking apart—so we can be pretty ferocious about protecting these fragile creatures. Hence stealing bread, and killing the person who stole my bread.

I want to draw our attention back to something I said a moment earlier about our sense of possession, of ownership of things. Property is our sense of self, extended beyond our skin. How we encounter the things of our lives, particularly those we feel to be "ours," is the ultimate spiritual discipline. How we treat things informs how we are as individuals, and becomes the basis for our engagement with the whole of the world. How we deal with things, particularly the things we see as ours, is the pivot point, the meeting of self and world.

Theft: A Love Story is the title of a novel by Peter Carey. If the things of our lives are the nexus, the meeting point of self and other, of our sense of self and our sense of oneness, well, theft is in fact a love story. We desire. We long for. We need. We want. Things. Food. Shelter. Attention. Others. No one is an island. And this longing, desiring, needing and how we engage it is the meeting of the sense of separation and the sense of oneness.

The practice, however, is to hold this all in a creative tension. We need to loosen up a bit. (Ain't that always the truth?) Start by letting be what is. Appreciate things as they are. Bread as it is. A pen as it is. A person as she or he is. Encounter our longing for each other and the world as it is without hasty action. Engage with appreciation, rather than mere grasping, mere accumulation, mere aggrandizement.

From that point we can deal with the harsh realities, with the person who can't get any bread and the other who has so much it spoils. But we need that wider perspective at the beginning. It opens our hearts and gives us the vision we need. There's an old Japanese proverb: Without action, vision is a daydream; without vision, action is a nightmare.

In the beginning of the nineteenth century, there was a Zen monk, a poet of some renown, named Ryokan. After his formal training ended, he returned to his home village. Just outside of town he built a small hut and took up residence. He particularly liked it because it had a lovely view of the countryside and the sky loomed large. By our standards he had nothing. But actually he had a lot. The villagers thought he was holy and they made sure he had food, and when he looked too ragged they gave him clothing.

Well, one day he returned from a walk and found a thief inside his hut. The thief was just leaving, having seen nothing he wanted to steal. Ryokan told him to wait, that there must be something the thief could use. Ryokan rushed inside and saw there really wasn't a lot. But he did have a blanket. He grabbed it up and he pushed it into the thief's hands, apologizing for not having more. The thief, embarrassed, clutched the blanket and ran away.

That evening he sat inside his hut, looked outside the window, and inspired by his wealth, wrote a poem.

> The thief left it behind:
> The moon
> at my window.

Understand this: have the moon and you will be rich beyond all reckoning; you will have the vision, and everything you do will be a blessing.

Do Not Misuse Sex

▪ RESPECT OUR BODIES ▪

> Treating all beings with respect and dignity, I vow to take up the Way of Not Misusing Sex. Self-nature is subtle and mysterious. In the realm of the ungilded Dharma, not creating a veneer of attachment is called the Precept of Not Misusing Sex. The Three Wheels are pure and clear. When you have nothing to desire, you follow the way of all Buddhas.
>
> ▪ BOUNDLESS WAY ZEN PRECEPTS CEREMONY ▪

1.

FROM THE BEGINNING of Buddhism, celibacy has been held up as one of the highest moral aspirations. It is encouraged among the laity; in the Vinaya, the monastic rule, it is mandatory, and the violation of this precept calls for immediate expulsion from the order. Within the Vinaya code, even a monk's unconscious ejaculation during sleep is considered a violation that requires confession before the community.

It is likely that the emphasis on sexuality is informed by the second of the four noble truths—often formulated as "the source of suffering is desire." And what stirs desire, burning longing in the human body and mind, more than sex? There should be no doubt about the power of sex and sexuality. It can be overwhelming, all-consuming, for both men and women, although in general perhaps more so for men. Even the projection of sexual desire can be astonishingly intoxicating. We can see how historically, across cultures, men's projection of sexual interest onto women has been the cause of much suffering for women.

And we need to notice how this may be the precept that has undergone the greatest shifts of perspective since it was first articulated in the Buddhist tradition; its reception within Zen communities today, particularly in the West, is complicated.

As a deeply human issue, how sexuality is treated is one of Buddhism's greatest shadows; how, despite its deeper teachings of radical interdependence, and its constant focus on the importance of being here now, at the same time a dualism persists between the body and the spirit. This can be seen in the way monasticism is deemed superior to lay life and the often harsh sexism that informs, and to my mind poisons, the monastic rule itself.

As Zen evolved within Chinese Buddhism and then migrated to those countries within the Chinese cultural hegemony, its handling of sexuality barely shifted. Robert Aitken says he surveyed the range of koan literature and found a single case that addresses sexuality straight on, koan 162 in the collection called *Entangling Vines*, "An Old Woman Burns Down a Hermitage," and some advice from Dogen, the founder of the Soto school in Japan and perhaps Zen's greatest theologian, cautioning people to avoid sexual gossip. And that pretty much ends the list.

Otherwise it would seem sex doesn't exist. That it is, sex didn't seem to exist until scholars noticed how rampant it actually was in Japanese Zen temples; as one example, both heterosexual and homosexual encounters were common among monastics outside the formal training periods. An even more morally complicated example was how young novices often wore long hair and makeup and were the objects of sexually inspired conflict among the older monks. As the temple system led to single monks occupying temples in the tens of thousands across the country, consorting with concubines quickly became normal; finally, in the nineteenth century, this aspect of sexual conflict was formally acknowledged and mandatory celibacy was eliminated in Japanese Zen.

Today, in our contemporary culture, while the subject continues to be confused and people have considerable difficulties in engaging either sexuality in our culture or their own sexual desires with anything approaching clarity, things are better than they have been in most cultures over the many years.

As we turned our attention to sexuality within Buddhism, and particularly Zen Buddhism, there were so many assumptions that had to be addressed. Right at the start: the relationships between women and men, and the related challenges to the assumptions of male superiority. Next: the fact of homosexuality, and with that the whole range of sexualities that naturally occur among human beings, and how to deal with these things in an open-hearted and open-minded way, which really is a manifestation of the awakened heart, the awakened mind. Even monogamy as the gold standard of human sexual relationships is not absolutely certain, as contemporary advocates of polyamory argue. What is certain here is that very little is certain—other than the fact that our human sexuality is more complex than we are often led to believe.

Against this background we're called to address our own sexuality, our own presence as sexual beings, and how we carry this into our lived lives. These are the questions of where the rubber hits the road.

There are institutional problems. The number of sexual scandals that have wracked Western Zen communities are too numerous to name here. There is a generally agreed upon assumption that a Zen student should not be subject to sexual invitations from Zen teachers. I certainly agree with that—and I think there is more room for conversation about the gray areas than is generally acknowledged at this moment in our history.

But what about the rest of our lives? In this Zen way, where our practice extends out into the broad highway of life, where we are not automatically expected to be celibate, what does this precept mean? What does it mean to desire without desire? How do we live our lives on the way fully, as sexual beings?

My friend the Zen teacher Diane Rizzetto, in her lovely book *Waking Up to What You Do: A Zen Practice for Meeting Every Situation with Intelligence and Compassion*, calls this precept "taking up the way of engaging in sexual intimacy respectfully and with an open heart." I suggest that may well be the key for us as we live our lives fully embodied, fully caring, with respect for ourselves and for each other.

This is a call to the way of the wise heart.

ll.

For reasons we've only begun to touch upon, as a matter of course most people don't handle the subject of sex well, and religion tends to be caught up in that confusion. I'm not sure of the whys of this. But I suspect it has to do with how sex reveals that we're in fact animals, like all other animals. And for some, for most, that's a problem.

Let me tell you that story I just alluded to from that great treasure trove of world spirituality, ancient China. Like many of the best stories, its origins are lost in the mists of time. There's a version of it in the Japanese koan collection *Entangling Vines*, which dates from the eighteenth century. But in fact this story is vastly older than that. It's one of those stories that has been kicking around in various forms for ages and ages.

I actually stumbled upon it in one of the very first books on Zen I would read, right there at the beginning of my serious spiritual quest. I was probably seventeen years old and, as I recall, nearly drowning in a sea of hormones. The book was Paul Reps and Nyogen Senzaki's little anthology of spiritual stories, *Zen Flesh, Zen Bones*. It may not be too much to say of the little story I found in that book that it reoriented my life. Or, at the very least, planted a seed that would grow in interesting and important ways.

Once upon a time, somewhere far away and a long time ago, there was a woman. She'd worked hard all her life and, while she had wanted to devote time to the spiritual quest, in her youth a marriage had been arranged. By the time our story begins she was a fairly well-off widow with an infant.

She decided to invest some of her money into spiritual work by supporting others in their practice, as a memorial to her late husband. She built a small but comfortable hut on her property and then invited a monk famous for his meditative prowess to take up residence as a hermit. She also provided food and drink and, when he was ill, arranged for a physician to visit. Otherwise she left him to his spiritual disciplines, which mainly consisted of silent meditation, sitting and witnessing the rising and falling of heart and mind. A good discipline; one I personally endorse. And one that the woman herself had learned, and even tried to do as often as she could.

The days and weeks turned into years. And at some point she began to wonder about her investment. She was, after all, a woman of business. She decided the best way to check the matter out was to ask her daughter—now in her full flowering of adolescence and who had been charged for several years with bringing food and drink to the monk—this next time, after setting down the tray with his breakfast, to put her arms around the monk and to whisper into his ear, "How does this feel?"

Let me stop for a moment. Up to that point, the only stories about sex and religion I could recall were from the Bible, and they all, like the stories of David and Bathsheba, and Samson and Delilah, tended to turn out badly. So I was pretty sure this would, too. Also, the act of sending one's daughter off to tempt someone offends our contemporary sensibilities. And in some versions of the story, the older ones, the girl is quite young. Trying to mute that complexity, I've told versions of the story with different characters of different ages doing the hugging. But this is in the spirit of the original version; a bit raw, a bit rough. We're talking about sex, and maybe the uncomfortable part of this needs to be part of the telling. Sex, you may have noticed, has shadows. And they extend all over the place.

Back to the story. The daughter, being a dutiful child, agreed. She took the tray, walked down the path to the hut, and set the tray on the small table outside the hut that she'd put many, many trays on many, many times before. Then she walked over to the doorway of the hut where the monk was sitting in his traditional cross-legged posture, meditating. She knelt beside him, threw her arms around him, and whispered into his ear, "How does this feel?"

He had been gazing at the ground a few feet in front of himself. Now slightly startled he raised his head, oh maybe an inch or two, looked into the middle distance, and replied,

> An old tree on a cold cliff;
> Midwinter—no warmth.

The young woman returned to her mother and reported all.

As I first read this, I thought, okay, the goal of the spiritual life described in this ancient Chinese story is pretty much like that of every other story I'd read: if you love God, cut off desire. Become, as one later writer would say, a "eunuch for Christ." But then the story took off in another direction.

Hearing her daughter's report, the woman was incensed. She muttered, "Sixteen years I supported that old fraud!" She grabbed a broom, stormed down to the hut, and beat the monk near senseless before driving him off. She then ordered the hut burned to the ground.

In Zen practice, when the story is told, the teacher will then ask the student "Why did the old woman burn down the hut?" This is a question that presents something about reality and invites us, you and me, to respond intimately. That's why this is a spiritual story.

But at seventeen when I first encountered this tale, I was flabbergasted. This wasn't right. This wasn't how it was supposed to go. My idea of sex and religion up to that time was that, if you want to be a spiritual person, sex has to go. Even my brief flirtation with a form of Hindu spirituality agreed with that assumption. Sex is bad. Sex is something dirty; at best it's something like going to the bathroom, necessary but still nothing you talk about in polite company.

At that time spirituality was something deeply important to me. I craved meaning. I craved knowing God or reality, that being or state or whatever it was supposed to be that religions promised. And, in the same instance, I burned with desire. I felt my sexuality and I burned hot. My heart was divided between two great longings. And the chasm between these two things was a tear in my heart. Then, here, in this little story, suddenly I was being confronted with a whole different question, working from a completely different set of assumptions. Here, it was pretty obvious, an ancient spiritual story was telling me that someone who didn't burn with desire was failing as a spiritual being.

Some years later I would find a poetic comment on this koan by the renowned Zen master Ikkyu Sojun.

> The old woman's kindness was like lending a ladder
>   to a thief;
> Thus, to the pure monk she gave a girl as wife.
> Tonight, if a beautiful woman were to entwine
>   with me,
> A withered willow would put forth fresh spring
>   growth.

In some translations that withered willow's sprouting is even more—how do I say this?—graphic. Clearly, clearly, here was—here *is*—a naturalistic spirituality calling us to be fully engaged with who we are. This is not an advocacy for libertinism. Absolutely we need to understand constraint, we need to know time and place; we are called to growth and depth and the miracles of change. But you cannot start any of that without knowing who you are. Any "should" has to follow "what is."

We need to know ourselves. We cannot practice Zen, a spirituality of presence, without bringing our whole selves into the great matter. That which is part of us, and which we deny, will inevitably return to haunt us, a hungry ghost of our night longing. And nowhere is this more true than in how we encounter our sexuality.

Our invitation on this way in every aspect of encountering ourselves and the world is to not turn away. Here it is just as true, if a bit more in one's face. As we open ourselves, our hearts, and from this perspective allow our bodies to be bodies, we will find the ways of restraint and letting go that become a joyful dance within reality.

The way is broad. The way is vast. And there is room for all of us, exactly as we are.

Do Not Forget Your Family

I commit myself to a culture of nonviolence and reverence for life; solidarity and a just economic order; tolerance and a life based on truthfulness; equal rights and partnership between people of all sexes and genders; and stewardship of the Earth.

■ THE FIVE COMMITMENTS ■

1.

The quality of mercy is not strain'd,
It droppeth as the gentle rain from heaven
Upon the place beneath: it is twice bless'd;
It blesseth him that gives and him that takes

■ WILLIAM SHAKESPEARE, *THE MERCHANT OF VENICE* ■

THERE'S AN OLD JOKE, originally told I believe by Emo Phillips; perhaps you've heard it.

> I was walking across a bridge one day, and I saw a man standing on the edge, about to jump off. So I ran over crying out, "Stop! Don't!" "Why not?" he replied. "What is there to live for?" I said, "There's so much!" Then he asked, "Like what?"

I said, "Well, are you religious or atheist?" He said, "Religious." I said, "Me too!" Are you Christian or Jewish?" He said, "Christian." I said, "Me too!" I asked, "Are you Catholic or Protestant?" He said, "Protestant." I said, "Me too! Are you Episcopalian or Baptist?" He replied, "Baptist!" I said, "Wow! Me too! Are you Baptist Church of God or Baptist Church of the Lord?" He said, "Baptist Church of God!" I responded, "Me too! Are you Original Baptist Church of God or are you Reformed Baptist Church of God?" He said, "Reformed Baptist Church of God!" I said, "Me too! Are you Reformed Baptist Church of God, Reformation of 1879, or Reformed Baptist Church of God, Reformation of 1915?" He said, "Reformed Baptist Church of God, Reformation of 1915!" I yelled, "Die, heretic scum!" and pushed him off the bridge.

Mohandas Gandhi famously noted that while he liked Jesus a lot he wasn't all that fond of the Christians he'd met. Of course this sort of thing isn't just for religious folk. I care a lot about those issues that fall under the rubric "social justice," but when I think of some of the social justice activists I've known in my time, I really understand what Gandhi means. A beautiful ideal can be badly handled by its supporters. Truthfully, over the years I've heard "Die heretic scum!" at meetings focused on one issue of justice or another a few too many times.

But I persist. And there's a reason. I suggest we may share that reason, you and I who walk the way of wisdom, who seek the wise heart. You've heard it before. It is the good news that is proclaimed in the silent places of our being: we are all in this mess together. This sad, terrible, glorious, beautiful mess: this is it. There is no other place. And the most important part of this realization is that you and me and the whole blessed world are actually one family.

II.

Consider the following story.

Once upon a time, long ago, and far away, there was a lovely little village nestled on the shores of a large river. The people lived simple lives, tending their fields and producing some handicrafts that were traded down the river for small luxuries. They were good and generous people, pretty satisfied with their lot.

And so when a baby was seen floating down the river, it was obvious that the very first person to see the baby would leap into the water, swim out, grab the child, and carry it back to the safety of shore. The villagers gathered together and examined the baby; she seemed to be in good condition, other than that thing about floating alone in the river. They decided that, until someone came along to retrieve the child, one of the village families would take the baby in. Frankly, one more would hardly be noticed.

The next day the villagers saw another baby floating down the river. So they saved him too. The day after that, two babies floated down. Again they took the children in. Well, this continued; each day more babies came, until the village had all it could do to keep body and soul together while tending to the many babies that they saved from the river. It became hard and distressing work. Still, they kept to it. But most distressingly, no one ever came to claim the children.

Finally, they agreed they needed to find out what was happening upstream. This is a dangerous moment. The work of saving those babies is astonishing; it is no mere putting of Band-Aids on problems. It is saving babies. It is seeing the need and taking care of those in need. It is good and holy work without a "but" or an "and." There is, however, a "still."

Perhaps you're familiar with Dom Helder Camara, a Roman Catholic bishop in Brazil during the twentieth century who was nominated for a Nobel Peace Prize. He once observed "When I give food to the poor, they call me a saint. When I ask why they are poor, they call me a Communist."

Giving food to the poor is saintly—and, but, still, at some point we also need to ask why there are poor among us. Why are people hungry and homeless, ill-educated and lacking adequate medical attention? Why are those babies being thrown into the river? Asking why is a dangerous moment, no doubt. In this little story the villagers decide they need to know, desperately need to know. They select six of their finest and strongest young people, three men and three women, give them a supply of food, solid walking sticks, good hats and sturdy shoes, and send them off to find out why these babies are being thrown into the river.

Months pass. Finally all six return. And everyone celebrates—well, everyone but one rather fat pig. But they do want that report. And they get it. It turns out that as the band followed the river upstream, after some miles it split into three tributaries. They created three teams of two to follow the branches. Each team had its report.

The first team said that after some hard, hard traversing they came near the head of the stream and there they found another village. There was something distressing about the people in that village and so they stayed hidden in the woods that ringed it, watching and listening.

It quickly became clear what the problem was. Each individual in the village was only looking out for themselves. They all ate as much as they could at every meal, and never once, at least while they were being watched by the visitors from downstream, shared so much as a bite with anyone. They also stole from each other. They would take anything not nailed down. It seemed they felt anything that wasn't for them individually was actually morally wrong. Of course babies were too much trouble, and so they just threw them all into the river. The young woman who had watched them said, "I've never seen such greedy people in all my life."

The second team had similar difficulties getting to the source of their stream, and they too, when they found the village near its source, felt that sense of unease, so also watched from a hidden vantage point in the woods.

It quickly became clear what the problem was. Each individual in the village was either angry with everyone else, or afraid of everyone else. They would slink around, avoiding anyone they could. And when they were forced into an encounter, it almost always ended in violence. Afraid their babies might someday harm them, they threw them into the river. The young man who had watched said, "I've never seen such hateful people in all my life."

The third team had the same difficulties, and the same intuitions, and also hid in the woods surrounding the village at the source of that stream.

It quickly became clear what the problem was. Each individual was so certain of their opinions that they would listen to no one else. Everything in the village had collapsed as each person refused to deal with anyone, no matter how trivial the question. They each knew everything, and no one believed anyone else. Certain that throwing babies away was right, they tossed them into the river. The young woman who had watched them said, "I've never seen people so certain of everything in all my life."

We are one family. But, sadly, we're a seriously dysfunctional family. We treat each other like strangers, when the truth is that we're all related. Wherever we are on this globe, we belong to the same immediate family; other animals are first cousins, trees and plants second cousins, and viruses and bacteria, well, they're no more than fifth cousins, once or twice removed. The air and the dirt, well, they're family, too, although I don't think our branches of the clan have been on speaking terms of late.

Flesh of the same flesh, blood of the same blood. And out of that knowing a spiritual ethos arises. Thomas Paine, in his *Age of Reason*, said it succinctly: "I believe in the equality of man; and I believe that religious duties consist in doing justice, loving mercy, and endeavoring to make our fellow creatures happy."

The call of the heart is to come home. And just recognizing our connections with each other and the world isn't really enough. The great project is to make that invisible intimacy visible, to bring it to manifestation and action. There are many ways, although the universal current is that "sitting down, shutting up, and paying attention." Social engagement, service and action, is a particularly important option for us on this path of realization. Social justice is the most powerful of disciplines calling for not knowing. The call is to struggle, not knowing how it will turn out, not knowing if it is of any use at all. Just not knowing. Not knowing until our hearts break and we discover the world beyond our selfishness and our isolation. Here in our vulnerability, in our broken-heartedness, we are given a great gift. In our raw presence to the whirlwind, we discover who we are. Here we find the one family.

At this moment the world is healed. And, sadly, in a moment, we will forget, and with that forgetting the hurt returns. That's just the deal. And so the project continues. There will always be another law to be challenged or enacted. There will always be another hungry person, a person who needs clothing, another who needs shelter. *Practice* is a magical word. It means both preparing and doing, both at once. But in that action heaven is revealed, hurt is healed, and lives are transformed.

I admit I'm personally attracted to what are sometimes thought of as larger projects, such as national health care, seeking marriage equality in my home state or helping push the national priorities to include global warming concerns and fair and humane immigration as well as racial and gender justice. I like the thought of possibly shifting our larger communal perspectives, if only a little. Such things stir my heart. But, you know, there is nothing like actually making sure someone isn't going to bed hungry today. So giving time to working at a food pantry, I believe without a hint of hesitation, can be the most important of social justice projects. This is justice rendered to its core without affectation or inflation. As would be volunteering with a hospice. There are many such ways to be of use that truly are manifestations of the work.

Whatever project you may consider joining, I hope you will consider joining one. For anyone hoping to walk a genuine and whole spiritual path, I believe it a very important part of our lives, of seeing deeply into the way things are, and seeing our part in it, both to the ill and for the good. I believe with all my heart that as we open our hearts, as we commit our hands, we discover the world transformed. Whenever we recall how our spiritual duties consist of doing justice, loving mercy, and endeavoring to make our fellow creatures happy, we discover the ways of healing for ourselves and for the whole world.

This is what we're about.

Do Not Drink the Wine of Delusions

Cultivating a mind that sees clearly, I vow to take up the Way of Not Intoxicating Mind or Body. Self-nature is subtle and mysterious. In the realm of the intrinsically pure Dharma, not giving rise to delusions is called the Precept of Not Intoxicating Mind or Body. Drugs are not brought in yet. Don't let them invade. That is the great light.

■ BOUNDLESS WAY ZEN PRECEPTS CEREMONY ■

1.

THE SIXTY-SEVENTH CASE of the *Book of Equanimity* is brief.

> The *Huayan Sutra* says, "Now when I look at all beings everywhere, I see that each of them possesses the wisdom and virtue of the Tathagata, but because of their attachment and delusion, they cannot bear witness to it."

Here is the promise of original awakening. We are told by the wise that from before the creation of the heavens and the earth all are awakened. This is our original face. But, most of us just don't notice it. Or, as Patrick Dennis tells us through his fictional Auntie Mame, "Life's a banquet and most poor suckers are starving to death." Or, in Hakuin's *Song of Zazen,*

> How sad that people ignore the near
> and search for truth afar,
> like someone in the midst of water
> crying out in thirst,
> like a child of a wealthy home
> wandering among the poor.

We usually receive this precept as "Do Not Give or Take Intoxicants." I understand the Chinese version is "Do Not Give or Take Wine" or, in the transmission documents I received through Jiyu Kennett, "the wine of delusion"; I think that adaptation is a clarification of the intent in the precept. In its literal form it is a call to us to not do those things that cloud our minds. And for many of us that literal precept can be life saving.

But there are all those other ways of investigating and understanding and manifesting this precept; that's how it can be a koan. Each of us possess, are possessed within, or simply are original awakening. And, yet, because of our attachments and delusion, we cannot bear witness to it. This is just terrible.

Here we are invited to look at the practical obstacles to our seeing who we really are. We need to attend to how it is that we cloud our minds. It can be drink or drugs; it can be television or the Internet. It can be how we see ourselves; it can be how we see others. On the most basic level, we're called to look into our own hearts and actions and see what it is that we are doing that clouds us, that turns us away from what is, from that promised original place.

A ministerial colleague and dear friend, Dr. Walter Weider, once told me he was going to start a school of pastoral counseling. Knowing Walt, I said, "Don't care for that nondirective stuff we're all trained in?" He gave me the baleful look that read "yes." Then he said, "It will have four areas of instruction. The first is *You What?!*, followed by *That's the Most Disgusting Thing I've Ever Heard!*, then *Cut that Out!*, and finally *Don't Ever Do That Again!*" Perhaps you have to come from the liberal religious tradition to see the humor in this. But, I think, it points to some aspects of this way of precept.

We are, I am sure, originally blessed. And, we, through our thoughts and actions, foul it up—sometimes really, really foul it up.

Often the solution is to just not do it any more, whatever "it" may be. As Dogen is thought to have said, "Drugs have not yet entered in, do not let them enter in. That is the great light." Once gone, the clouds are gone. And if you have let "it" in, well, stop. And if that seems too hard, well, then stop anyway. Once gone, the clouds are gone.

And if that doesn't work, seek help. There's lots and lots of help. I love AA and all its variations. And zazen; just looking hard sometimes is enough. Although it usually means also checking in with someone you can trust who will hold your feet to the fire.

Once gone, the clouds are gone.

And if you don't have a big life-disturbing problem, don't get too smug. The delusions we swim in are the stuff of our ordinary lives.

So cut it out. And if you can't cut it out, cut it back. And return to the cushion. And seek out those friends. Know that no one ends up doing it on their own, even as we must all do it for ourselves. That's why it is a conundrum; that's how it becomes a koan.

There's one more point in the koan of clouding our lives: clarity and clouding, ultimately one thing.

See through this, and all the koans are answered. That is the great light.

//.

As do they all, this precept has at least three aspects. There is that literal one: don't drink. There is the essential, the absolute, the empty, the boundless: here the drink and emptiness are one thing. And there is the compassionate: that moment where the great empty and the totally ordinary meet, birthing the play of our lives.

Within that truth we discover how we were born for joy. I repeat: we were born for joy; that state of happiness, felicity, and delight that is our common birthright. I know how it can seem contrary to what we may have experienced in our sense of separateness, of isolation, in the face of such sadness as many of us have had to endure. However, even within our isolation we can almost always feel a seed of knowing there's something more. We find it in our longing for another. We glimpse it in all our desires. The longing itself suggests something we might yet find.

Of course we too often confuse the matter. We have a thirst and we think that, if we get that object of our desire, our thirst will be quenched. But it rarely turns out so. Too often, we can't put a stopper on the desire and it becomes compulsion—either for one thing after another or for one thing that we return to and return to—even though it never satisfies. Instead of joy we find frustration, and sadness, our sense of isolation confirmed.

Compulsion and addiction are those irresistible and persistent impulses to some action. Those who've been caught up in this experience know it can feel like it comes from outside of us. And it can be overwhelming. Much hurt follows when we confuse this longing for joy, for connection, for knowing our true selves with some object outside of us: sex, or drink, or drugs, or, well, I suspect you can name it for yourself.

But here's the rub. Those objects of desire and the brief, transient ecstasy that they bring can under some circumstances point you to an intimation of the great joy, to a leap beyond obsession with ourselves to a place that is our experience of connection to each other and the great world. A persistent metaphor for this knowing is intoxication, a divine intoxication. This encounter is the pearl of great price; it is our own personal discovery of that joy for which we were born.

To be clear: I'm not arguing that drinking too much beer on a Friday night will lead you to enlightenment. And in fact such transient ecstasies can just as easily carry you to the brink of great suffering. But the flush, the bonhomie, the heightened sense of ecstatic companionship with friends and strangers, can serve as small whisper reminding you that we are all one, that we are born for joy—and that the real and difficult and sober spiritual work is worth doing. That there might be a path to a joy that is fluid and a constantly renewed discovery that what we should call "ourselves" does not end with our skin.

So while knowing there are dangers involved, considerable

dangers—my own family and the hurt and death that followed depression and addiction bear witness to the dangers—still, considering intoxication as a key to a deeper knowing can be worth reflecting on. In fact, I think, we need to.

Every culture knows intoxication, both the sad kind and the joyful kind. And that's why in some—in fact, most—spiritual traditions we simultaneously find cautions and calls to our fundamental joy as a kind of divine intoxication. Among the Sufis in particular we find this divine drunkenness as a persistent image. But there are Jewish and Christian and Hindu and Taoist allusions to this, as well. The earth-centered traditions make much of this. Only the Buddhists seem for the most part wary of the use of intoxication as an image of that gateway. A caution we should be aware of!

The phrase *divine intoxication* describes the experience we all can have when we bring our separateness and our unity into our hearts, and it becomes how we see the world. Part of the power of the image of intoxication is that we have all seen what can go wrong, how dangerous intoxication might be, can be, is. We who have committed our lives to this spiritual enterprise, we all have our stories about this. Some are helpful, direct pointers. Others, well, perhaps they're more cautionary.

I came of age in the 1960s in the San Francisco Bay Area. This all by itself says a great deal about me, more than I can comfortably describe. One area at that uncomfortable edge was how those of us caught up with spiritual questions were as a group enticed toward drugs and religion, and particularly what I like to call techno-shamanism: reconstruction of the shamanic quest as a spiritual discipline. Or perhaps more honestly: getting high as a spiritual practice.

I was very much aware of what alcohol could do to people. My father's drunken haze throughout my childhood, and the dark consequences for us as a family, was something of a caution. But I was on the dumber side of the human intelligence spectrum at the time and I bought the fashionable rhetoric that while alcohol was stupid, pot was delightful, and LSD was sacramental.

The Beatles' *Magical Mystery Tour* was background music, Timothy Leary was in full hedonic swing, and backyard shamans everywhere were mixing up and offering shortcuts to mystical experience at very reasonable prices. There was even a whole literature emerging. In particular I'd read a lot of Aldous Huxley, including his two small treatises on psychedelics: *The Doors of Perception* and *Heaven and Hell*.

I was maybe eighteen when with a small band of friends I dropped acid for the first time. Within twenty minutes the world had taken on some very strange shapes indeed as we wandered through the Anthony Chabot Regional Park in the East Bay's Oakland Hills. I may not have been the sharpest tack in the box, but I quickly noticed the world was not as I'd previously thought. The wind sang, trees bowed, and the grass whispered. Instead of a walk along the surface of things, I'd fallen through the rabbit hole into some strange, very strange, wonderland.

All went pretty well until I looked up into the sky, and felt it open, and open. I peered into the dark night, even though it was a full-on California summer afternoon. I don't know if you've ever seen the old film *X: The Man With the X-Ray Eyes*, but suddenly I was Ray Milland, peering into the center of the universe and finding an all-seeing eye. An *unfriendly* all-seeing eye. I peered ever more deeply, beginning to fall into the eye, and despair began to envelop me, a smothering cloak.

And then a hand rested on my shoulder and a friend said, "Whoa, James. Look at this." I turned my attention from the sky, a twirl of light, and saw the small pebble resting on his open palm. I was entranced with its beauty. As William Blake sang: "To see a world in a grain of sand / And a heaven in a wild flower." Then the kaleidoscope shifted to something else. The next hours were a gentle walk through the park until the effects of the drug passed away with the afternoon.

Who knows why things turn out the way they do? For me this psychedelic adventure, although intense, was brief. I had persistent suspicions that chemicals weren't what it was about. What, after all, does a hobbit adventure, or even a malevolent eye watching all, have to do with melding into God, with finding the truth? I suspected strongly that what the mystics were describing—and I read them voraciously, despite Huxley's guidance—weren't the same things I was finding in psychedelics. And, so, I ended up entering a Zen monastery and sojourning among people who were not big on intoxication as a metaphor for awakening to who we really are.

A couple of years later when I returned to the world, as it were, the psychedelic era had disintegrated; Haight-Ashbury, the cosmic center, had become a denizen for speed freaks and heroin addicts, and a very dangerous place to visit. The whole enterprise appeared to have fallen into madness, and as far as I was concerned the techno-shaman experiment had failed. I admit I have friends who beg to differ.

And, to be honest there was one legitimate lesson I learned from the spiritual use of drugs, and that was that the world, indeed, is not how we normally think it is. That is an important lesson.

But that's the only spiritual teaching drugs offered me, and I suspect, all they offer anyone. And, truthfully, you can find the same lesson by just sitting down, shutting up, and paying a little attention to what's going on.

We were born for joy. And everything is an intoxicant. Everything. Whether it be a pebble or a grain of sand or a friend or a lover or a bottle of wine. However, there are two kinds of intoxicants: those that diminish us, and those that expand us.

And—this world is so complicated in some ways—the truth is each thing may be either. And sometimes both. So use caution. Be careful. We need to live our lives in a dangerous world. But, if we are careful, and if we are just a little lucky, as we give our attention to what is in front of us, strange and beautiful things can happen.

May I suggest, for us, for you and me at this time and this place, the best way to throw ourselves wide, to find that divine intoxication, that joy which the universe has promised us from before our parents were born, is simple enough.

Master Dogen once observed in his commentary on the koan of everyday life that when we advance toward the ten thousand things, that is simply delusion—when we look at the world through our prejudices, or our intoxications, that is missing the mark. Rather, the deal is to allow the ten thousand things to advance to us, inform us, expand us, open us wide. I suggest this is a rather different project than one normally finds within the drug experience.

This way to which we are invited is about opening up, not shutting down. It is not about abnormal experiences, but the most ordinary of them all, just this, just this.

The world revealed.

Our very selves revealed.

Afterword

For the listener, who listens in the snow,
And, nothing himself, beholds
Nothing that is not there and the nothing that is.

■ WALLACE STEVENS ■
"THE SNOW MAN"

A FEW YEARS AGO I visited the Zen center which at that time was in upstate New York, led by Margaret and Mui Barragato, teachers in the White Plum lineage. I'd been invited to give the Dharma talk, but it was the liturgy that caught me. Pretty much the standard Soto thing, except it was enriched with a couple of items from the Western literary canon. What caught me was how well Wallace Stevens' "The Snow Man" worked. And this enriching is not all that uncommon. John Tarrant has folded Rainer Maria Rilke's "Ninth Duino Elegy" into the liturgy celebrated at his retreats. And my own Boundless Way community is currently exploring what Western texts might best support our liturgies.

A lot of water has flowed under the proverbial bridge since I first sat at the Berkeley Zendo those many, many years ago. Everything there was done in Sino-Japanese, the Japanese liturgical language, pronouncing Chinese in the Japanese manner. When Jiyu Kennett arrived from Japan in the late 1960s and established her sitting group in San Francisco, it was considered a novelty, and perhaps something over the top, to actually translate the Heart Sutra into English. Philip Kapleau experienced similar reactions on the other coast as he introduced English texts, just translations of conventional Zen texts, into the Rochester liturgy.

The roots may be tentative, but drawing together the wisdom of Asia and Europe and increasingly Africa, here the Zen way is definitely taking on a new shape, perhaps incorrectly called—for lack of a better term, which may yet come—a new and Western shape. It's now been about twenty-five hundred years since Gautama Siddhartha preached his great sermon, turning the Wheel of the Law for us all. And now there are new encounters. The ways of Buddhism, for me most importantly the Zen schools, have had their own meetings, confrontations, encounters and challenges here in the West. This time the meetings are with Christianity, Judaism (a side note: I learned most all my Yiddish living in the Zen monastery) and other currents of Western religion as well as, and probably equally important to all the others together, Western psychology. Already we are seeing some of what that encounter is going to lead to.

I learned to read sitting with my grandmother holding her big old King James Bible on her lap. Moses and Miriam, Jesus and the Marys live in my dreams. In my adolescence the richness of the Western Enlightenment and its ultimate flowering within the scientific method seeped into my bones and marrow. Now, with decades of zazen under my belt, having met the entire koan curriculum as transmitted through Daiun Harada, his disciple Haku'un Yasutani and their heirs, and having read into the Dharma, particularly its Zen expressions, for forty years, all of this brought together within this old skin bag, I cannot say where one strand of who I am ends and another begins.

What I can say is this: if your heart is broken, if you find a longing that cannot be satisfied in the ways the world is offering it through secular culture, come to a Zen hall.

Come just as you are. No need to be someone else.

Sit your butt down.

Shut up.

Pay attention.

Learn who you were from before the creation of the stars and planets.

Investigate the ways of differentiation.

Explore the geography of not knowing.

Become.

And forget.

And become again.

And, then when you get off that pillow—for goodness' sake—do something.

This becomes the dance of becoming where the stars take their course, and planets teem with life and death and life again.

It can manifest as healing for your own heart, and it can reveal a way of healing for this poor, beautiful, broken world.

Indeed, it almost certainly will.

Acknowledgments

WRITING ACKNOWLEDGMENTS is an impossible enterprise. There simply is no way to note everyone who makes something like a book possible. Yet still, we must try—and there are names that absolutely need to be named.

First, I need to name my teachers along the way, formal and informal. There have been many—but here I want to hold up my ordination master, the late Houn Jiyu Kennett and my koan master John Nanryu Ji'un-ken Tarrant. Running a deep current behind them are the lines of Soto Zen and Soto Zen's Harada/Yasutani koan reform movement.

I also want to acknowledge the deep influence of my collaborators in the Boundless Way Zen school, and particularly Melissa Myozen Blacker, David Dayan Rynick, and Josh Mu'nen Bartok, who did double duty as my editor at Wisdom Publications—an enormously difficult task that he managed with grace and aplomb.

There are various Unitarian Universalist communities that I've had the honor of serving, all of which have contributed to who I am. I particularly want to acknowledge the congregation of the First Unitarian Church of Providence, within whose warm embrace I wrote this book.

The wonderful folk at Wisdom deserve numerous acknowledgments. I want to thank freelancer Phil Pascuzzo for the delightful design of this book and Laura Cunningham for her editing skills in assisting Josh Bartok in bringing this project to fruition. Laura is also the person who suggested the title for the book. Lydia Anderson, Wisdom's marketing and promotions person, has gone beyond the call of duty in trying to share the merits of my project, for which I am deeply grateful.

Lastly, I want to thank my spouse Jan Seymour-Ford, a true person of the Way, friend, and lover. Friends who know have said I would never have become a Zen teacher without her. They're right.

James Ishmael Ford
Benevolent Street Zendo
Boundless Way Zen
Providence, Rhode Island

Index

About the Author

JAMES ISHMAEL FORD has been a prac-
ticing Zen Buddhist for over forty years.
He has degrees in psychology, divinity,
and the philosophy of religion. He
ordained as a Soto Zen priest and
received Dharma transmission from the
English Zen master Houn Jiyu Kennett. He then continued
his training in the Harada-Yasutani koan tradition, com-
pleting formal training and receiving inka shomei from the
Australian Zen master John Tarrant. He is the founding
abbot of the Boundless Way Zen network and continues to
serve that community as a guiding teacher.

James is also a Unitarian Universalist minister. He served
congregations in Wisconsin, Arizona, and Massachusetts
before coming to Rhode Island, where he currently serves
as senior minister of the historic First Unitarian Church of
Providence.

A prolific writer, James is becoming one of the foremost
proponents of an emerging liberal Buddhism in the West.
He has contributed to the Buddhist magazines *Buddha-
dharma* and *Shambhala Sun* and is a columnist for the online
edition of the *UU World*, the principal publication of the
Unitarian Universalist Association. His popular blog, the

award-winning *Monkey Mind* is hosted by the religious portal Patheos.

He is the author of *Zen Master WHO?*, a history of Zen Buddhism in North America, as well as co-editor with Melissa Blacker of *The Book of Mu*, a detailed exploration of Zen's foremost koan.

James lives with his family outside Providence.

About Wisdom

WISDOM PUBLICATIONS is dedicated to offering works relating to and inspired by Buddhist traditions.

To learn more about us or to explore our other books, please visit our website at www.wisdompubs.org.

You can subscribe to our e-newsletter or request our print catalog online, or by writing to:

Wisdom Publications
199 Elm Street
Somerville, Massachusetts 02144 USA

You can also contact us at 617-776-7416, or info@wisdompubs.org.

Wisdom is a nonprofit, charitable 501(c)(3) organization, and donations in support of our mission are tax deductible.

Wisdom Publications is affiliated with the Foundation for the Preservation of the Mahayana Tradition (FPMT).